LOST IN THE WEEDS

An Introduction to Legal Issues for
Business People Leading Cannabis Companies

JOSHUA ASHBY

ATTORNEY AT LAW

THE REFERENCE GUIDE TO WASHINGTON STATE RECREATIONAL MARIJUANA LAW

ACKNOWLEDGMENTS

There are many people to thank for helping with this book. Christopher Larsen's contributions were central to the success of the project from start to finish. His insight as former Editor-in-Chief of the Seattle University Journal of Environmental Law was essential throughout the writing and editing process—furthermore, as one of the most knowledgeable recreational marijuana attorneys in Washington State, his legal understanding about I-502 was indispensable.

Highwater Press especially thanks Avitas Agriculture, Inc. for their immediate enthusiasm about the project when I first mentioned the book. Avitas also provided generous financial support. In particular, thank you to Adam Smith, CEO at Avitas, for his insight into the industry as one of the most successful producer/processors in the State of Washington.

A special thanks for important contributions made by Gary Ashby—a person without any prior knowledge about I-502. He patiently listened for many hours and asked the questions that filled the gaps in the explanations Chris Larsen and I sought to provide.

Thank you to all the clients who provided direct content for the book, including: Jason Smit at Avitas Agriculture, Inc.; Alex and Becky Hutton of Seattle Sound LLC; and Craig Fitzgerald from The Root Cellar LLC. I also appreciate the many valuable conversations with Fadi Yashruti at Seattle Inceptive Group LLC, dba Suspended Brands.

Thank you to assistant editors Caitlin Ashby, Kellie Piña, Matt Kelly, and Lindsay Larsen. Thank you also to I-502 attorney and contributor Sean Badgley.

I also express appreciation to all of the clients who provided an opportunity to acquire the expertise that made this book possible. The second edition of this book, including revisions and additional content, is already underway as this book goes into publication—I welcome criticisms or suggestions to help make the next edition better. Send emails to: blowback@highwaterventures.com.

Photo Credit: Highwater Media

HONORABLE MENTIONS

Special thanks to Alison Holcomb—who is often described as the "Architect of I-502." Her lectures during various events at the inception of this project were foundational to the legal understanding that made this book possible—on several occasions, her explanations clarified some of the most challenging legal doctrines related to this area of law.

Likewise, Chris Larsen thanks Stephanie Boehl for sharing her insight with those who attended the CLE she chaired—the resources she provided were helpful in preparing his early contributions to this book.

TABLE OF CONTENTS

part four

VOTER INITIATIVE

part five

THE LIQUOR CONTROL BOARD

part six

WHERE ARE YOU GOING?

part one

WELCOME

WASHINGTON STATE EXPERIMENTS WITH RECREATIONAL MARIJUANA

Most people with any connection to Washington's recreational marijuana industry will eventually go foraging for an industry guidebook. Ironically, some of the troublesome issues arise from relatively straightforward situations—so straightforward in fact, that there may be no guidance just yet because no one else has dealt with the particular problem before now.

Alternatively, the large number of blog posts, online forums, or Google groups may present an overabundance of information, from many sources, that merely sifting through all of the conversations and threads in order to find the most reliable, current information may be a problem.

Everyone in this industry has felt lost in the weeds at some point—the longer you've been here, the more likely you've already been mixed up at some point. Don't get too discouraged by unforeseeable setbacks—I haven't met anyone who hasn't had at least a few.

For those of you just starting to explore the feasibility of an opportunity to invest in a marijuana business—this book is written specifically for you. Lost in the Weeds was written in direct response to the disappointment many clients expressed when they were getting started in the industry. The truth is, when an industry's complete revenue history is still counted in months rather than years, in temporal terms, everybody is new and opportunity is abundant. That said, the learning curve has been steep and missteps sometimes measure in the hundreds of thousands.

This book covers setbacks and problems that have recently occurred and the questions raised during our initial conversations with clients regarding Voter Initiative 502, codified under the Revised Code of Washington 69.50 (RCW 69.50) and the Washington Administrative Code 314-55 (WAC 314-55)—commonly referred to as "I-502." Companies operating under I-502 are often simply called "502 companies." If you need help with an obstacle that you've encountered while navigating the cannabis company landscape—you've come to the right place. This reference guide will get you pointed in the right direction.

INTRODUCING VOTER INITIATIVE 502

This reference guide is a great place to start your recreational marijuana industry historical research and the specific laws here in Washington. Whether you're an investor, real estate developer, attorney, farmer, interested entrepreneur, closet herb grower, or existing licensee, this book will be a valuable resource for getting oriented with I-502.

Lost in the Weeds will simultaneously be totally eye opening and reveal whether or not this is your cup of tea, or project a sense of confidence and vision of the business potential and venture opportunity that is within your grasp.

This book is not intended as a comprehensive legal treatise. Instead, this is a legal primer on the subject of recreational marijuana in Washington State. In fact, in many ways this is the primer for a whole discussion about I-502 and the laws in Washington. At the time when this book was written there was no other comprehensive reference guide in publication that dealt so specifically with the law governing recreational marijuana in Washington State.

Many books out there deal with medical marijuana, such as issues of production, processing, scalability, or any one of the various other technical aspects of growing, selling, and smoking weed. But *Lost in the Weeds* focuses instead on the specific laws here in Washington related to operating a legal, licensed recreational marijuana business—this should be a helpful starting point or a place to get oriented if you're already underway. If you don't find what you need in the following pages, check out some of the additional resources mentioned throughout the book.

THE VALUE OF MONEY

Selling Nickels and Dimes

Investing in an I-502 operation is a lot different from managing an operation—there is no shortage of the former, but fewer are well qualified for the latter. Finding an investment opportunity in the industry, for now, is as easy as attending the next local Meetup.com event for some cannabis related topic (for more information visit www.RedRussak.com or tweet @RedRussak). The challenge, like any seed capital investment, is accurately assessing the likelihood for success.

Although, general investment advice is outside the scope of this book, there are a few issues to keep in mind that are specific to the recreational marijuana industry here in Washington. Such opportunities are plentiful because many business owners are finding that they need more capital as the start-up phase continues to be more expensive than was initially anticipated. Consequently, some business owners may face insolvency and have begun failing—unable to move forward without additional funds.

Fortunately, the opportunities to find funding are also plentiful. Many people are realizing they missed the pot boat a year ago, so now the only option may be to give some of their money to one of the already established, though struggling, businesses that are desperate to succeed.

As with any nascent industry, there are potholes, and you must figure out whether this industry will be a good fit for your style of investment—going through this book is a great way to start. As important as knowing your own style—find out whether the company you are considering for an investment shares your basic philosophy on business or other core values that may be important to you.

Are they a company that is interested in skirting up against some of the rules, or are they more conservative with their approach? It is important to invest in a company that will not jeopardize your interests. This has been one of the primary reasons we have clients coming to our office for advice. Many businesses have reached the transition point where outside investment is a necessary next step for the company's growth plans.

Consider the following: the original owners have brought the company as far as they can go; let's assume they started with $200,000. Now they are at a point where they need several million dollars to move forward. Enter the sophisticated investors. The investors are coming in from outside the company and they will likely want and require formal business documents and specific provisions to protect their investment and interest in the company.

There may be securities laws affecting whether the company can begin soliciting money and before the company may legally accept money from an outside investment source—including whether a new investor can join the venture.

"I KNOW A GUY"

There are no typical investors—especially not in this industry nor is the situation likely to change soon—like the many different strains of cannabis, any number of factors may emerge as the dominant characteristics defining a potential investor. The potential for high returns attracts investors, but, it's more than just that—this is an investment in recreational marijuana. It's cutting edge. It's fresh, new, even a little exciting and untapped. It sounds impressive.

It's important to keep in mind that not every investor is going to have millions of dollars. Or perhaps more importantly, investors who are interested in investing in a marijuana business may be unaware of the overall costs involved. Often times a new investor or client interested in the industry is one who has the technical expertise but lacks business or financial expertise.

An increasingly common type of investor that recently joined in is the more cautious, discerning, individual who has been waiting for more stabilization within the industry—such investors may have a great deal experience or little to no experience at all. This investor is typically someone that has done well personally and may be bringing anywhere from $100,000 to $500,000. They want to remain completely passive but require specific investment formalities—for example, requiring operators to secure their loan with personal assets.

As the industry becomes more standardized and widely accepted, rather than the shady unpredictable black market, you are going to see an even wider variety of people who are seeking to invest. Rather than investing in a lackluster mutual fund, they say, "I see this marijuana business and I would like to be part of that. I can't get my own business or I don't want to run my own business but I would love to take on a little bit of risk myself and hopefully see the payoff."

PRICING AND VALUATION

Many people's first question about the industry will focus on seeking to understand the risk of an investment in an I-502 business. Most recognize that the risks to return extend beyond a company's business model or anyone's business acumen—evaluating the investment risk must necessarily include some awareness of the legal factors affecting a company's ability to continue operating uninterrupted.

For investment valuation purposes, companies have primarily used a discounted cash flow method—including companies that have neither completed the final permitting process nor reached first revenue. Revenue multipliers for valuation purposes have been ranging from as little as 2.5 to as high as 8 in some cases; often depending on the successful record of accomplishment that the company has been able to demonstrate.

In an industry that is so new, valuation by comparison is difficult—if not impossible—because guideline companies are practically nonexistent or represent too small a sample to be reliable. Even the earliest startups are still in their infancy. Asset focused valuations have also been infeasible, so far, because—despite assets of equipment and improvements largely undepreciated—many feel the numerous hurdles from an I-502 company's inception to revenue cannot yet be appropriately estimated due to the tremendous variation among license applications, site locations, and a constantly changing legal landscape across state, local, and federal jurisdictions.

According to estimates by the Washington State Liquor Control Board (WSLCB, also commonly called the "LCB"), around half of all I-502 businesses are expected to fail within the first twelve months of operation. If that proves true, failing to perform an adequate due diligence investigation will be like investing thousands, or millions, on a coin toss. In my experience to date, the statistical success of clients has far exceeded any flip of a coin—but they also represent a self-selecting subset of business people with enough foresight to be working with business planning attorneys.

INDUSTRY INSIGHT:
A NOTE ON SELLING SECURITIES
Sean Badgley, ATTORNEY AT LAW

As of this writing, the state and federal governments are still trying to solve a very basic issue. How can lending institutions loan money to cannabis businesses? While the authorities figure it out, entrepreneurs are opening businesses that require capital to operate. Those in the industry usually decide to sell a stake in their business and in exchange for capital (equity). When one sells equity, she is actually selling a "security," which is (broadly speaking) an investment instrument.

The Federal Government, specifically the Securities and Exchange Commission (the SEC), regulates the selling of Securities. Although most small and medium sized businesses don't have to worry about the SEC, the nature of this industry means that a wise licensee or applicant will take a moment to check regulations because the SEC has acted against marijuana businesses in the past.

The first thing licensees and applicants must figure out is whether they need to even consider the SEC. Typically, when someone goes out to raise money (sell equity), she contacts close friends, business partners and associates, and asks a few individuals to fund the project. As a general proposition, if someone is going to get money from a few close people, those people are simply business partners. So, for example, if someone has an LLC with a license, but wants to expand, the person with the license could offer to sell 25% of their LLC to a friend for capital. The parties can negotiate over the deal and the friend could simply become a "member" of the LLC, a "shareholder" in the case of a corporation, or a partner of some other sort for different entities by signing a contract and handing over a check.

However, many projects require a large amount of capital, and it may simply be easier to raise small amounts from many people, rather than large amounts from a few investors. If an applicant wishes to take this approach, then she will be making an "Offering." Offerings have several important aspects. If you think your plan to raise money might be considered an Offering, you should immediately consult a Securities attorney, because there are several important rules in place one must follow. For instance an applicant is limited (but not prohibited) from certain types of negotiating between investors, because generally speaking, every possible investor needs to have access to the same Offer.

The second consideration is whether the applicant needs to "register" with the SEC, or whether the Offering is "exempt" from registration. Usually, cannabis Offerings are exempt.

However, the applicant still must "file" for the "exemption." Once again, expert lawyers can assist you with this process, which is very straightforward. No one expects even the savviest of applicants or licensees to know how to complete all the steps necessary to follow the SEC rules. However, it is smart to take a moment to determine what the Company's strategy is for raising capital. An hour with an expert (even one who bills at hundreds of dollars an hour) is a wise investment that will ensure the business doesn't run into problems before it even starts spending the money the licensee worked so hard to raise.

WHY MARIJUANA?

While growing marijuana sounds like a lot of fun, without an adequate business strategy—it won't be fun for long. Anyone hoping to harvest more than one crop should remember that a business must at least cover its own expenses, let alone be profitable, in order for the business to remain in operation.

For an investor who once romanticized the idea of owning a vineyard, but quickly sobered after a closer glimpse or look—it may be easy to understand the appeal of owning and operating an I-502 company for many of the people who now hold pending applications but lack the resources to move forward. Just like a vineyard, which requires much more than a refined palette for sampling wine—starting up, managing operations, and earning a profit will require more than simply rolling joints. If your primary objective is to have legal access to as much weed as you want, owning, investing, or operating an I-502 company is an expensive way to go. If you're thinking that you'd be satisfied to simply break even that perhaps the joining like-minded people in the I-502 business community is more appealing than the economic aspects of the company—you should seriously consider looking elsewhere to earn some cash, then buy all the weed you could ever want at a legally-licensed retail location. Consider for example that although sampling your own product is allowed—such allowances typically are small and must be traced and reported to the State. Marijuana is never allowed to be consumed onsite at any I-502 licensed facility. If you owned a vineyard, at least you could eat a few grapes.

COMPETING INDUSTRIES

Pharmaceutical industries have shown they're concerned about the emergence of marijuana as an industry. Even though marijuana first came out or got a strong foothold in its medicinal applications, it is much more analogous to the beer, wine, and alcohol industries—craft beer might be the best analogy. The artistic element of a marijuana grow operation is more like growing hops or operating a vineyard. It is the cultivation of plants more than the mixing of chemicals.

There is also the processing and retail aspect of the I-502 industry—edibles, concentrates, and vaporizer pens. When you're dealing with edible products, labels are crucial to minimize liability. In part this is due to the lack of standardization, albeit a common problem in many food industries. It is important to find out that one cookie six inches across may be ten servings and not the one serving it might appear to be.

Think of the last time you read a nutrition label on your favorite snack; the entire package may contain four servings.

The difference here is that instead of increased consumption of calories, a person is dealing with increased consumption of THC. Make sure you know the product's serving size and what it means. Do not hesitate to ask the retail associate questions. Often times the retailer or sales associate has an interest in the industry and are very knowledgeable about their offered products. Ask questions.

Education is a huge component of the recreational industry. This industry is no longer limited to the black market where a consumer is limited to whatever product is currently available. You now have resources for education on the product—to learn what exactly you are buying and determine which product best suits your needs or wants. A lot of people who are involved in the industry are enthusiastic and more than willing to share the knowledge they have. It is not uncommon for people who have been in this industry on the illegal side for many years to now be operating legally and enjoying the fact that they can speak about it without having to conceal their involvement.

Edibles may or may not be something that people have been exposed to before. Consumers may be using concentrated cannabis oil, which means it may be stronger than either edibles that they have had before or that they have made and eaten at home. The intoxication or impairing effects may be much stronger.

The LCB has begun to address some of these traits in edibles and has recently adopted many more specific rules, such as homogenization. Homogenization means to make uniform or similar. It is the idea that a chocolate bar with four servings has an even disbursement of THC in each serving. Previously, a four serving chocolate bar could contain almost all the THC in a single serving, which could have severe side effects.

Homogenization in milk, for example, is when you do not end up with a carton of milk that is nothing but fat, which would generally float, or nothing but water in another carton. Homogenization tries to create a consistency of the fat percentage in the milk. It is the exact same thing for edibles and THC.

The market for edibles remains in flux. Some in the industry expect edibles to maintain a stronghold, while others expect interest to wane. The argument against edibles is simply a lack of desirability. Who wants to simulate a candy bar or cookie when you can have a drop, concentrate, or lozenge and then have a real candy bar?

Alternatively, edibles succeed largely because they are developed off of what would otherwise be waste—marijuana trim. Because processors have created a commodity out of waste, it is unlikely that this market will go away.

Concentrates, just to add a little bit more information here, come in a couple varieties. You have oils, hashes, waxes, kief, and amber glass. If marijuana was compared to a light beer, then concentrates would be a stiff whiskey drink—they are strong and they have a quick effect. Users should begin slowly because concentrates are affected by variables such as body weight. You cannot necessarily rely solely upon the experience of someone else.

Vaporizer pens are another consumable that many people are less familiar with as they are relatively new. They are quickly emerging as one of the most popular methods—it is heavily concentrated because they are made with the marijuana extract. A vaporizer pen is comparable to an electronic cigarette.

In terms of places for consumption, public versus private, Washington State law protects the private consumption of marijuana, meaning that you can openly consume marijuana in a residence as long as the property owner allows it. Note that it does not necessarily extend to someone who is renting the property. There may still be a lease in place, which expressly prohibits (and is legally enforceable) any controlled substance, which is based off of federal controlled substances laws. Make sure that wherever you're consuming marijuana, the property owner allows it, not just the resident.

Marijuana cannot be consumed in any place within public view, such as streets, sidewalks, or public parks.

Marijuana also falls under the state's ban on smoking in public places, RCW 70.160, which prohibits smoking of any kind in a public place, including any place of employment. In terms of a hotel, it's analogous to tobacco. Smoking in any indoor location is subject to the restrictions of Washington's smoking in public places law, which prohibits smoking in public places or places of employment, or within twenty-five feet of an entrance, exit, windows that are open, or ventilation intakes that serve an influenced area.

A final comment on places of consumption—outdoor activities are traditionally some of the most popular opportunities for consumption, such as boating, hiking, and skiing or snow-boarding, etc.—however, bear the following in mind before choosing to consume any-where other than on private property or in a private residence.

According to the US Coast Guard, if you are in navigable waterways (navigable waterways having a somewhat murky definition), assume this includes all bodies of water) they will enforce federal law.

Possession of marijuana remains illegal under federal law. That means on a boat, a ferry, or on Lake Washington for Independence Day watching the fireworks, possession of marijuana is illegal. Additionally, operating any vehicle while impaired by marijuana or any other drug is clearly illegal. Federal law also applies in national parks and the state law against marijuana use in public view applies to state parks, public hiking trails, and ski resorts.

INDUSTRY TRENDS AND PROJECTIONS

One of the most obvious reasons for the widespread interest in Washington's marijuana industry is the potential for profit.

The hype is hard to dismiss when the state is forecasting over a billion dollars in taxable revenue during the first five years (see Washington State Economic and Revenue Forecast, June 2014).

Even more recently, estimates from data in the monthly reports, which every I-502 company must file, predict revenue may actually be three-fold above original expectations—exceeding $3 billion.

Note these projections apply solely to Washington State's closed loop market.

If these forecasts are correct, the resulting tax revenue could range from $250 to $750 million.

If these numbers sound high, as they originally did to me, consider by way of comparison that in Washington State revenue from beer and wine approaches $15 to $20 billion every year.

This leads my next point—competing industries.

There are huge out-of-state funders opposing voter initiatives on the matter. In most instances, it is not the local people or the not-in-my-backyard movement who are mobilizing oppositions to legalization. Rather, it is out-of-state money coming into Washington opposing the legalization of recreational marijuana because at some point they will be ceding their own market share.

We have determined, at this point, it is difficult within a nascent industry like this to find out which industry really parallels it. Where is the model? What is the recreational marijuana business model based on? We have settled on beer and wine—not hard liquor—as the most analogous to the marijuana industry.

It seems like a strange proclamation today but many business owners and investors in the industry expect to see marijuana move further away from the black market and become more accepted by society. Perhaps a more likely new consumer is a person who enjoys a glass of wine at night to wind down or as they get ready to go out for the evening.

There are marijuana strains that have been bred specifically for that "winding down" effect. The stronger forms are better for insomnia while milder forms would serve a similar purpose as a glass of wine. Alcohol is often used to reduce stress and many strains of marijuana are designed to have the same effect.

The bottom line is that marijuana still faces the stigma of being an illegal substance—it is still a Schedule I controlled substance under the Federal Uniformed Controlled Substances

Act—but many are projecting that this may slowly transition to widespread national acceptance with increasing legalization.

part two

Death & Taxes

TAX: BALANCING OBSTACLE AND OPPORTUNITY

Excise Tax

Taxes usually come up during most discussions about changing marijuana laws. The potential tax implications of the changing marijuana law is a popular point of discussion in much of the public discourse.

There's a saying about death and taxes, these two things are for certain and recreational marijuana is no exception to this saying. Business owners across the I-502 industry have been outspoken over the twenty-five percent excise tax and the system of taxation that Washington has adopted.

The burden of the issues that will certainly be addressed and that causes issues with pulling marijuana out of the black market is the taxes and other fees that create the recreational market. We should qualify here and say that Alison Holcomb (ACLU and "Architect of I-502") does not agree that taxes are too high. Rather, the problem is the tax structure—the twenty-five percent excise tax is not problematic, it is simply in the wrong place.

What are the Tax Implications?

Many people base their entire knowledge of the industry on their limited exposure to what is reported on the televised evening news. People may know there's a twenty-something percent tax, but little or nothing about how it is implemented. Much of the national media coverage has been focused on Colorado because they were quicker in the implementation between voter initiatives to retail sales.

Many people have no idea that the state laws even vary, let alone any knowledge on how Washington's approach departs from Colorado's. This is especially problematic when such people enter the public discourse with the wrong information seeking to sway decisions on anything from rezoning to an outright moratorium of all business activities.

The first thing many people say is, "Yeah, pot is going to be taxed at twenty-five percent," which doesn't seem like that big of a deal at first, especially because we're talking about switching the product from illegal and "shady" to legal and sought after—people are not really as concerned.

People may hear something along the lines of: "it is still illegal federally" and they come in to consult with the impression that there is some illegal enterprise tax that makes it impossible to succeed. This is Internal Revenue Code (IRC) Section 280E, which is coming up for the first time with the first end-of-the-year financials for companies that started operating in 2014.

Business Person Perspective: "I heard that they were going to enforce that (IRC 280E), so if they enforce it, what's the incentive to start operating legally? When I look at it, I look at it from an average guy who might say, 'Hey, I would not mind investing in this, since banks can not lend.' That's the other thing that seems counter-productive. It is hard to get financing, and harder still to have any sense of security with your money when federal banking laws leave your local branch squeamish to take a deposit from a marijuana company."

THE COST OF 280E: TAXABLE INCOME

This provision exists under Internal Revenue Code 280E placing an even heavier tax burden at the federal level on top of the 25% excise tax here in Washington State. When the 280E provision appeared over 30 years ago, it was aimed at curbing the profits of black market businesses—tax liability beyond net income to all but cost of goods sold. Without a doubt, profits will be curbed across an already nascent I-502 industry.

The immediate effect will be to further dull the competitive edge of companies legally operating under constant scrutiny by state government. Ironically however, the people defeated by this tax regime are the people we hope might have a fighting chance at taking on the black market's reign on marijuana. And perversely, that same provision whose inception was designed to combat the black market will now help to insulate it from challenge by a legitimate market still struggling for financial viability—so for now, it looks like Washington's recreational industry will be going to this gunfight with a spoon.

Although the stance on marijuana today is relaxed to the point that its prohibition is not enforced federally where it is otherwise legal, however, the IRS continues to utilize 280E as a source of revenue even though the intended purpose of 280E, combating the black market drug trade, no longer serves as its function.

Taxpayers in the medical marijuana industry have attempted several strategies to cope with 280E. Some taxpayers operate multiple trades or businesses and allocate expenses liberally to those trades or businesses that allow for deductions. In the tax court case Olive. v. Commissioner, 139 T.C. 2 (2012), taxpayers in a medical marijuana retailer were unsuccessful in an argument that the taxpayer provided care-giving services as a separate line of business and that some expenses should be associated with this business.

A similar argument was successful in the case Californians Helping to Alleviate Medical Problems v. Commissioner, 128 T.C. 173, (2002), however, the taxpayers' primary feature was care-giving services and marijuana dispensing was secondary.

Other taxpayers requested a Private Letter Ruling from the IRS that would have approved of the business as a 501(c)(3) tax exempt organization. The IRS did not agree that the company was formed for charitable, religious, educational, and scientific purposes because a single substantial non-exempt purpose destroys the exemption, and federal law deems the activity illegal and does not recognize the medical benefits of marijuana. Some have argued a 501(c)(4) tax-exempt organization is a viable option, but such an opinion has been met with resistance.

A more successful strategy is to maximize the capitalization of expenditures into inventory. Under IRC 263A, producers of tangible property must include in inventory the indirect costs as well as the direct costs of producing that inventory. Inventory costs are a cost of goods sold so they offset gross income without regard to 280E.

For instance marijuana producers can potentially capitalize seed expenditures, planting costs, cultivation costs, irrigation, pruning, soil and water conservation, fertilizing, frost protection, spraying, harvesting, upkeep, and electricity. Indirect costs that can partially be allocated to inventory include purchasing, handling, warehousing, security, cost accounting, data processing, production coordination, legal, and accounting costs.

The portion allocated to inventory offsets gross income over the course of years. Ironically, the taxpayer may rely on years' worth of capitalization-friendly rulings and regulations issued by the IRS because it is generally in the interest of the IRS to advocate for capitalization rather than expense.

STATE V. STATE: NEIGHBORHOOD DISPUTES

Another popular news topic is the diversion of marijuana into neighboring states. How is it addressed when people come to Washington to buy marijuana and then leave across state lines? What are the issues with policing it in states that still prohibit marijuana? At this time there are no answers for these questions.

BEING NEIGHBORLY

Consider the following hypothetical example. Say you observe a house that, in the past, has had a marijuana grow operation. You might have seen, at all hours of the night, all kinds of random strangers come and go. It is quite the opposite for a licensed marijuana producer/processor location. They are not going to be entertaining all types of random people beyond business hours. Unless you went online and were targeting a specific location, I do not see how one would necessarily know the location of a marijuana producer/processor operation.

The purpose is not to cater to the public. Consider the idea that we all know where to go to buy groceries—our favorite local grocery store—but how many of us know where the products sold come from? Do we know the location of the specific orchard in which our apples are grown? Could we easily stumble upon that exact orchard? The brand is provided on products sold in grocery stores but that still does not indicate exactly where the product originated. The impact to your neighborhood could be undetectable.

CRIME RATES

Returning to the idea that legalizing marijuana is, hopefully, going to reduce or eliminate the criminal element, how is the cash issue resolved? You have a cash based industry with nowhere to protect the money—banking is an issue. Many federal banks don't want to touch "dirty money," leaving local banks to take extremely large risks. Does this present a new arena for crime? Are these new businesses high crime targets?

An equally concerning and related issue is that of banking. How is the state going to handle this situation? If the demand for product is high and operations need more capital, what are their options? Is private funding their only option? Colorado has explored opening a state backed bank to manage the capital needs of grow operations. Locally, a few credit unions have offered banking services to I-502 operations.

Area Crime Rates

Another common misconception is the likelihood a criminal is going to break in to a store or trespass on growing fields and steal the marijuana product(s). Although the recreational marijuana industry is still new here in Washington, there are places where comparable track records has been established—based on medical marijuana operations, there is no difference between what criminal elements may be introduced by a medicinal marijuana grower versus a recreational marijuana grower.

While the news and TV has sensationalized the idea that homes with marijuana operations have been burglarized for the crop and money, the statistics have actually shown the criminal element has declined, albeit not eliminated altogether. Merely because there is some crime that is being committed, is not necessarily an indication that crime has risen in the industry. Generally, the crime trend has been declining.

More Misinformation

When dealing with the community, public meetings are a common place for concerns to be voiced. When attending these meetings, or when talking with the neighbors, you need to inform them about the security measures you have put in place and the attempts to keep the property aesthetically pleasing. The first thing most neighbors would want to know is who will be drawn to the operation with concern for the valuable property and marijuana's historically cash based (untraceable) transactions.

This is a common concern raised by a lot of neighbors but often a misconception. It is actually quite shocking how much misinformation is out there. When neighbors learn about the level of security required for licensees, with a plethora of the other mandatory requirements placed on businesses in the industry, most rational concerns should be eased over the risks that someone will be free to simply wander into a I-502 operation and take marijuana.

Similarly, given the strict transportation and sale procedures imposed on licensees, these businesses will not be rampant with shady visitors. Rather, like any industry, the only people regularly seen on the premises will be the employees.

PRODUCERS/PROCESSORS AND RETAILERS

Keep in mind there is no retail element for producer/processors. Even for retail locations, there is no consumption allowed by the public on the premises or by the people who work there. Producer/processors cannot even test their own product on the business property. All product tests are to be conducted on private property.

MEDICAL MARIJUANA

Brief Synopsis of Medical Marijuana

With regard to the content of this book, there is not much to compare between medical marijuana and recreational marijuana laws, because the medical marijuana industry is more or less unregulated. For example, both Seattle and Tacoma, the first and third largest cities in the state respectively, have said they are not going to allow medical marijuana without a state license. The problem here is that there is currently no state license in existence for medical marijuana.

It is contended that this is purely a response to the challenges faced in the recreational industry, which will have trouble succeeding so long as marijuana thrives in both the black market and the medicinal market. Washington and Colorado enacted recreational marijuana in 2012, but it was in 1998 that Washington permitted the use of marijuana for medicinal purposes.

GROWING RIFT: MEDICAL AND RECREATIONAL

How does this coordinate or reconcile with medical marijuana? It is commonplace in the news to hear about the accessibility of medical marijuana and dispensaries are seen all over the state. Is it known how the state will address this conflict? The medical marijuana industry lacks most of the regulations felt by the recreational industry and many are unsure how this conflict will be resolved.

Currently this is a hot topic with the state legislator and many bills are being considered during the current legislative session. It can only be postulated at this time, but some speculate the medical marijuana industry will be rolled into recreation, while others believe stricter regulation will be put in place for medical marijuana production and sale.

LOCAL MEDICAL MORATORIUMS

The restrictions presented by Seattle and Tacoma to medical marijuana raises an interesting point with regard to local prohibitions of recreational marijuana and that is simply the question of whether or not this is permissible. Current lawsuits are pending which will address this very question. On the one hand, it is contested that this was a state approved statute, voted on by the people.

While on the other hand, there is the federal prohibition question whether a state can force its counties to permit the use of marijuana. A related issue is how the counties have drafted its land use provisions to control where marijuana can be produced, processed, and sold. This highlights the single biggest issue we have dealt with in the industry, finding a suitable location for a marijuana business.

OPPOSITION FROM OLD RIVALS

Political Power of Petroleum, Cotton, and Tobacco Wanes

If you go back to the time when marijuana was first made illegal, three of the most powerful industries in the United States were its biggest opponents. The industries were oil, tobacco, and cotton, all of which were threatened by the growth of the marijuana industry. Hemp threatened the cotton industry; the intoxicating effect of pot threatened the tobacco industry; and the oil extract threatened the crude oil industry.

This was during the early 1900s and given the powerful political presence within each industry, it is argued that this is part of why marijuana was made illegal during this time. Interestingly, those three industries have significantly waned in the United States during the past century.

Oil, for example, has moved mostly out of the United States and its popularity politically has waned in the face of global warming and the energy conservation measure. Likewise, cotton and the textile industries have moved overseas. Tobacco has been one of the last major opponents, but with all the health related issues and expensive lawsuits, it has also lost a lot of its power in combatting the marijuana industry.

THE NEW PUSHERS

Drug Makers and Alcohol Industry Favor Prohibition

In the interest of public health and safety, the law requires a warning of the danger posed by combining alcohol and pharmaceutical products to be featured prominently on both industries' product packaging and container labels. However, these two industries have been doing everything possible to block public efforts to legalize marijuana, including combining their alcohol and pharmaceutical companies' money and influence to block voter initiatives.

Perhaps one of the most interesting aspects of the legalization of marijuana is who opposes the movement. At first blush, one would think it is mostly conservative groups who fear legalization of marijuana would increase crime rates and use of illegal drugs. While this group certainly exists, as we previously discussed, and the arguments are not completely un-founded, we have found that many of the challengers to the marijuana industry are those well-established in the beer, wine, and pharmaceutical industries.

The challenges the marijuana industry faces will be directly driven by the beer and wine industry or by the pharmaceutical industry. Such challenges can actually be traced back to the early history of the United States, far before the Controlled Substance Act was established and marijuana was deemed as a Schedule I drug.

THE REFORMATION

Weed Law's Budding Prospects

There are three categories that are affected by the changing of the nation's marijuana laws: medical marijuana legalized, decriminalization, and recreational marijuana legalized. The first, medical marijuana legalization is the category most people are familiar with; however, it is beyond the scope of this book. There is an abundance of resources out there available online and in print.

Decriminalization, which typically results in no prison time or criminal record for first-time possession of a small amount of marijuana for personal consumption is an increasingly common approach. And finally, the focus of this book, legalization of recreational marijuana in Washington State.

LEGALIZED OR UNENFORCED

It is almost inaccurate to say that marijuana is legalized in Washington State. More accurately is the concept that marijuana is still illegal at the federal level under the Uniform Controlled Substances Act, but Washington State is not obligated to, and has chosen not to, enforce the federal laws.

part three

THE LAW OF THE LAND

THE UNITED STATES OF AMERICA: A FEDERAL GOVERNMENT OF LIMITED AUTHORITY?

Federal preemption is the formal argument people make when asking, "How can you legalize it in your state if it is still illegal federally?"

Even the United States Supreme Court has weighed in on this issue, finding that Congress may criminalize the production and use of home grown cannabis, even where states approve its use for medicinal purposes. There is also an anti-commandeering aspect to enforcement. They (the Federal Government) cannot commandeer state agencies to enforce federal law. To clarify, the Federal Agencies may enforce federal law within the states but the federal government cannot force state agencies to enforce the federal laws.

CONTROLLED SUBSTANCES ACT

If you're really new to this industry, you may be unfamiliar with the legality issues at the federal level. At the end of the 1960s the Controlled Substances Act was passed by President Nixon. The Act created classifications to designate various chemical substances into Schedule I, Schedule II, Schedule III, Schedule IV, and Schedule V categories.

Schedule I is the most relevant to our discussion. These are substances considered at high risk for abuse and with no medical or medicinal value whatsoever. This means that under no circumstances may they be used for research purposes, nor for anything else. Other examples of Schedule I substances include narcotics like heroin, certain forms of methamphetamine; MDMA (ecstasy); Lysergic acid-25 (LSD); and cannabis (marijuana).

Cocaine, by way of comparison, is a Schedule II substance. Cocaine is not a Schedule I drug because people used to believe it had medicinal purposes. They used to put it in Coca-Cola so you could feel better.

FEDERAL FUNDING

Marijuana's designation as a Schedule I substance is significant because it prevents state-run universities from conducting any research on its potential uses. As a result, it is difficult to provide any support for the medicinal benefits of marijuana because it is the big private universities that have the money to conduct the necessary research to show the benefits and risks.

When you are telling an investor about some of the risks, they must keep in mind that marijuana is still federally illegal and there's really very little protection, beyond the non-binding memos and budget measures, to keep the federal government from knocking down doors, seeing the marijuana and ultimately shutting down business.

It is not just the marijuana plants or buds, but any property that has been used in the production, distribution, or sale of the marijuana. In all reality, an entire marijuana business operation could be easily shut down by the federal government legally enforcing their federal laws.

FEDERAL TRENDS: 2014 OMNIBUS

It is important to point out that even though marijuana was addressed differently than it's ever been addressed before in the most recent federal budget, it does not mean it is going to stay that way. This is a one-year budget with three key points.

Federal dollars are no longer allowed to be used in the prosecution of individuals who are operating legally under state medical marijuana laws. In the bill, which is over 1,000 pages, they have a single provision that lists out all of the states in which federal funds are allocated to the Department of Justice and cannot be used to prevent states from implementing medical marijuana laws:

"SEC. 538. None of the funds made available in this Act to the Department of Justice may be used, with respect to the States of Alabama, Alaska, Arizona, California, Colorado, Connecticut, Delaware, District of Columbia, Florida, Hawaii, Illinois, Iowa, Kentucky, Maine, Maryland, Massachusetts, Michigan, Minnesota, Mississippi, Missouri, Montana, Nevada, New Hampshire, New Jersey, New Mexico, Oregon, Rhode Island, South Carolina, Tennessee, Utah, Vermont, Washington, and Wisconsin, to prevent such States from implementing their own State laws that authorize the use, distribution, possession, or cultivation or medical marijuana."

Basically, if it is legal under state law, the Department of Justice (DOJ) will not prevent implementation of laws that allow for medicinal marijuana use. It is important to note that this does not prevent enforcement against recreational use and it does not mean that in a neighboring state, such as Idaho in Washington's case, medical marijuana use is legal.

INDIAN RESERVATIONS

The second point clarifies the use of marijuana on Indian reservations, which are actually federal lands. After the budget came out, another memo was provided saying that federal Indian tribes are given similar treatment as the states—they are free to legalize marijuana.

Just like the states, they also need to draw up their own regulations that are going to prevent marijuana from getting out into other states, or leaving federal Indian land.

I think one of the big components of this treatment is that the federal government wants to create a relationship between the state Attorney Generals and these federal Indian lands and say, "Attorneys Generals work with the federal Indian tribes that want to legalize marijuana, and help them come up with regulations for their tribe that are going to prevent diversion off the reservations."

Probably not a perfect analogy, still, consider fireworks. We know that Indian tribes can sell fireworks on their land, and there is very little that prevents anyone, who is not an Indian, from going to a reservation, purchasing the fireworks that are illegal and having a great 4th of July back at their own place, off the reservation. Federally, they really want to do a better job making sure that if these tribes are going to legalize marijuana, the product and production is going to stay on their land.

It is a particularly sensitive issue with Native Americans because of the substance abuse problems that they have historically battled. There are really high rates of alcohol and narcotic abuse, and because of this, a lot of tribes are adamantly opposed to any form of legalization of any controlled substance on their lands.

The Yakima Nation threatened to sue throughout the State of Washington for the legalization of any form of marijuana. They might not sue the state for any marijuana legalization, but they were going to sue for production/use on any ceded lands—lands in the State of Washington that were ceded at any point in time.

With Washington being a territory that was unionized a little bit later, this is a significant portion of Washington State. Ultimately, the Yakima Nation backed down from that threat, and it's no longer an issue.

This raises an important point, Alison Holcomb, one of the authors of I-502, will tell you that the writing committee very carefully crafted the rules that were passed on I-502 so that the state does not in any way, shape, form, promote or require anyone to operate or proliferate any of the marijuana use.

Many people proposed that legalization should have followed how Washington had previously treated alcohol, with state-operated liquor stores. However, the reason that the state decided not to do that is to avoid overstepping the federal bounds, in that, now you would have a state employee working in a liquor store who essentially is required to violate federal law in order to perform their job duties.

The third point is counter to the legalization of marijuana, and that was Congress' decision not to follow the vote of the people to legalize marijuana in the District of Columbia.

THE COLE MEMORANDUM
James Cole, DEPUTY ATTORNEY GENERAL
August 29, 2013

The other point on federal law that must be discussed is the Cole Memo, Deputy Attorney General James Cole from August 29, 2013. This was significant and progresses along the same lines as the federal government pulling back their enforcement of marijuana laws. This memo laid out eight specific points that the federal government was going to continue emphasizing with its marijuana enforcement.

The Cole Memo really sets the backdrop to everything that is going on at the federal level right now because it sort of alleviates a lot of federal fear. If I were to talk to an investor, these are some of the things that, of course, they would want to know: "Can the Feds still come in and shut down these marijuana operations?" The simple answer is yes, but the Attorney General has provided some guidelines as far as what they are going to enforce.

It is worth mentioning that this is such a significant memo that some Limited Liability Company (LLC) operating agreements, in the state of Washington, have specifically referenced the Cole Memo in saying that, "This is how the company's going to operate, as we deal with federal law, see the Cole Memo and its eight points."

This is a memorandum, not an act of Congress—it can change as suddenly as political opinion. It is possible, for example, in 2016 that there could be a new memo with new guidelines—on the other hand, there could be no change at all. This is one reason I am not a huge advocate of incorporating a memo such as this into an Operating Agreement by reference. A presidential election is another possibility that may or may not affect the industry, it's something any investor should consider. It's a little counterintuitive, but despite the growing strength of the industry, obstacles of uncertainty are likely to persist for the foreseeable future. This type of risk is supposed to be reflected in the rate of investment returns that an investor will see. For instance, there are companies borrowing money at interest rates in excess of twenty-five percent—such high rates are due to the risk and uncertainty in the industry. Nevertheless, such risk has the potential to reap tremendous returns. An investor must simply weigh the alternative and balance the risk against return.

Going back to the Cole Memo, these are the eight points that the Department of Justice is still going to closely monitor and enforce when necessary.

1. Minors

Preventing distribution of marijuana to minors. As a side note, it is interesting to see the correlation between the Washington laws and the eight points in the Cole Memo. Colorado was far less conservative, and took what they're calling a Wild West approach. Washington took a meticulous approach in coordinating every step with federal government and saying, "OK, we are going to do this. Are you OK with it?" There was a back and forth between the state and federal governments, so Washington took a lot longer before they actually started issuing licenses. Washington's laws are very carefully crafted in terms of the regulations.

2. Financial

Preventing revenue from the sale of marijuana from going to criminal enterprises, gangs, and cartels. There is quite an issue here that the system is set up for failure. Specifically, there is an issue in the financial sector with taxes and banking. This is where the criminal elements—the cartels—come in, and where you cannot get something that you need to run a business. That is where you get the loan sharks and twenty-five percent interest rates that are usury. At this point, there are exceptions to the usury for implementation of the industry, and Washington does not have a usury restriction. Eventually, they are going to have to address those areas, because right now they are vulnerable to accounting and cash issues.

One of the advantages of working with a law firm like ours is that we add a degree of legitimacy—we help provide some of that traceability with funds. We have had clients who are able to bring large cash deposits and we can put those in a trust fund. They are then introduced into the banking system to file the reports and all that is necessary for compliance.

A very misguided, but not uncommon, question is whether you can you create a separate entity that operates like a financial entity for the company—one that can put the money in the bank and be used by the I-502 business. Laundering does not allow you to do that, because you have to follow the bad money. One of the biggest red flags you can throw out for yourself is to open up that separate company.

3. Across State Lines

Preventing the diversion of marijuana from states where it is legal under state law in some form to other states. This is the Colorado/Nebraska lawsuit.

4. Other Illegal Activities

Preventing state authorized marijuana activity from being used as a cover or pretext for the trafficking of other illegal drugs or activity.

5. Violence

Preventing violence and the use of firearms in the cultivation and distribution of marijuana.

6. Public Health

Preventing drugged driving and the exacerbation of other adverse public health consequences associated with marijuana use.

7. Intoxicated Driving

Preventing the growth of marijuana on public lands and the attendant public safety, and environmental dangers posed by marijuana production on public lands.

8. Federal Property

Preventing marijuana possession or use on federal property, which is one that has been recently addressed with regard to Federal Indian Land. A memo from Monty Wilkinson, the Director for the Executive Office for US Attorneys was released on December, but dated October, 2014, stated that Native American reservations could legalize marijuana in a similar method as the states—with coordination with the federal government and state Attorney Generals' office to assist with enforcement and to prevent diversion.

TRANSPORT AND SHIPPING

One other federal issue with regard to federal property is airspace. People will commonly ask, "Can you fly marijuana from Seattle to Spokane, or navigate the waterways?" Simply put, the answer is no. The Federal Aviation Administration (FAA) regulates all aspects of American civil aviation and the Coast Guard regulates all navigable waterways and original jurisdiction is granted to the U.S. federal courts by the U.S. Constitution.

Planes, Trains, and Automobiles

The key with FAA regulation is that it applies even when flying within a single state. There are all kinds of technical issues here, such as whether you stay below 500 feet or if you are using a non-pilot operation or ground controlled vehicle, but these are not gray areas that one should attempt to exploit. Admiralty law is really interesting in Washington State as we are surrounded by bodies of water and it is home to the largest ferry system in the world. Additionally, many residents live on islands.

For instance, one prime example is taking place on Vashon Island, in the Puget Sound, which has no bridges and state operated ferry access is the only regular way to get there. A huge investor put up millions of dollars for a state-of-the-art marijuana production facility, which was going to be located on Vashon Island.

It was only later determined that they could not transport that marijuana on any waterway and there was no way for them to take their weed off of the island. They would be free to produce and process marijuana for use on Vashon Island, but nothing could legally leave the island.

The inability to use airways is also tricky due to the geographic nature of Washington State. Eastern Washington provides ideal outdoor growing conditions, but much of the consumption would likely occur in Western Washington. Transportation is a challenge because there is no flying of your marijuana, for example, from Yakima to Bellingham. They have to transport it by truck. Keep in mind that this not only extends to transportation of mass quantities, but also samples that one business owner may want to provide to another in order to conduct a possible future transaction.

More companies are having difficulty getting through and finishing the licensing process because they cannot find a suitable location that they can take all the way through the complex process. This is something that comes up often at the licensing process. The companies have to explain how they are going to operate without violating any federal laws. For example, let's say you don't have to use the waterway or the airway, but the land you are interested in leasing is owned by the city port authority.

Ports often operate under the Coastal Zone Management Act (CZMA), which provides that states and local authorities have the jurisdiction to operate the ports or areas adjacent to waterways despite the fact that this area extends past the navigable waterway. The federal government provides permission to the city port authority so long as it complies with federal law.

The port is free to operate its land and provide for lease terms that will not jeopardize its right to manage the port, such allowing someone to clearly violate federal law by producing and processing marijuana. There are cases currently in litigation in the state dealing with this very situation.

UTILITY ACCESS: POWER HUNGRY AND THIRSTY FOR WATER

Power Hungry—Electricity

We have had at least one client who is in a county where the power being sold to the local utility provider is one hundred percent produced by a federal agency, Bonneville Power Administration (BPA) in this instance. They have no way of obtaining power from the public utility that is sourced anywhere else but from the federal agency. BPA is situated on the Columbia River and generates hydroelectric power that is sourced throughout the Pacific Northwest.

It is important to understand a little bit about the Federal Energy Regulatory Commission and how it is set up and how it moves through to the local level. Right now, electricity is produced by lots of different companies in lots of different places. The federal government is just one of the harvesters of energy. You've got an electrical grid and an open market. While in some markets the energy is deregulated, it is not a completely free market.

Normally, it is limited to three levels: the consumer, the wholesaler/utility, and the producer. Some utilities are also producers themselves. The county, which may be the utility, actually negotiates rates for certain industries that may consume greater levels of electricity, such as technology, and these rates will be very different from residential consumption or manufacturing.

For example, Mason County has responded to the issue that Bonneville Power Administration is a Federal Agency and may opt to forego providing power to I-502 businesses by designating a specific class for their I-502 companies. The county contends this is a good thing for the I-502 companies because if the county is forced to cease providing power to I-502 companies—as a result of the power originating from BPA—the county will have the freedom to find an alternate source of power for the designated class.

The county would not have this option if the I-502 companies operated individually, but power can be supplemented to the class as a whole if the BPA chooses to abide by Federal Law and prevent its power from being supplied to the I-502 companies.

It is possible that some counties may combine I-502 companies into an agricultural classification but it is important to note that under Washington law marijuana is specifically excluded from agriculture designations. Even though we refer to it as a crop and as an agriculture type commodity, legally it is not considered agriculture in Washington State. The huge distinction whether or not a product can be treated as agriculture ultimately has many implications.

The issue with the electrical power is that producer/processors are the ones who are the huge consumers of electricity. In many instances, they have to install additional transformers to connect with the grid, which may cost anywhere from $25,000 to $100,000 and additional lines to reach out to their rural location. If they are not allowed to use public electricity, there may only be one alternative: an onsite generator. Generating power is an option for an I-502 operation, but whether or not it is cost effective will vary by situation.

The important point to consider is just this, when looking at a location, you need to make sure that the utility providing electricity does not get one hundred percent of its power from a Federal Agency, like Bonneville, because if it does, you could potentially run into an issue.

Water Irrigation Rights

In the Western United States, water rights are a huge issue—Washington, less so than some other states like Colorado or California. However, especially in Eastern Washington, many water rights will also be shared or tied directly into Native American reservation rights, which are federal rights. A lot of farmers in Eastern Washington actually buy their water rights from local Native American tribes, which presents an issue.

If you buy one hundred acres in Eastern Washington, or any area where Native American reservations are commonplace, you better be sure you are not one hundred percent relying on irrigation that is coming from federal water rights through the Native American reservation, otherwise you risk being cut off. It should be noted that it is unclear how the recent shift towards legalization of marijuana on federal Native American reservations will impact these water rights issues.

My recommendation is that water rights is something you are going to have to account for and you need to be aware of what the potential risks are. If you have an alternate water source, such as a private groundwater well, you are probably going to be OK.

OTHER FEDERAL AGENCIES AND DEPARTMENTS

Here is a list of other potential agencies about which any I-502 or marijuana related business should be aware:

Drug Enforcement Agency (DEA)
Attorney General's Office (Federal)
US Patent and Trademark Office (USPTO)
Environmental Protection Agency (EPA)
US Coast Guard
Federal Deposit Insurance Corporation (FDIC)
Department of Transportation (DOT)
Federal Energy Regulatory Commission (FERC)
US Department of Health and Human Services
Center for Disease Control (CDC)
US Department of Agriculture (USDA)

INTELLECTUAL PROPERTY

Intellectual Property (IP) is arguably one of the most complex areas of the law when it comes to the legalization and distribution of marijuana. Not only do the terms frequently get misused, but also there is much confusion regarding the acquired rights and what rights are actually afforded to those operating in the marijuana industry.

It is commonly asked, "Can you get a patent or trademark on different varieties of marijuana?" As can be the answer to nearly all-legal questions; it depends. As with nearly all aspects of this book, it is important to seek the advice of legal counsel before proceeding with your venture or taking on any component described in this book.

IP can generally be broken into three major categories with two lesser known, but no less important, sub-categories:

> Copyright
> Trademark
> Patent
> Trade Secret
> Trade Dress

Plainly, federal trademark registration is not an option because of the Lanham Act, which provides the basis for trademark law and prohibits registration of marks that are "immoral, deceptive, or scandalous matter." Given that marijuana is still federally illegal, the United States Patent and Trademark Office (USPTO) considers marijuana trademarks immoral or scandalous.

However, the far less utilized option that is available is state trademark protection. For instance, an individual may obtain trademark protection by using the mark in connection with a good or service in commerce and by registering the mark with the state trademark agency. In Washington State, this requires the completion of a trademark registration form and submission of three samples—one of which must be an original as currently in use.

It is important to understand that state trademark protection is limited to the state in which the mark is registered. If the mark is to be used outside the state where trademark protection has been received, it will be important to seek protection in the new jurisdiction.

Patent protection is where things get more complex. It is first important to understand a bit about marijuana. An analogous industry that most are familiar with is the apple industry. There are many varieties of apples. For instance, there is the Fuji apple, Granny Smith, Honeycrisp, Gala, etc. These are all varieties of apples that any grower can produce (sometimes requiring a license). Marijuana strains—with equally unique names—are similar in the sense we think of apple varieties.

Take for example "Snoop's Dream"—there may be multiple producers growing Snoop's Dream, but it is not the strain that sets apart the product. It is the individual producer and the processes they have in place to control quality. Think of organic versus traditional farming. It is the trademark protection you can get for the brand, and not the strain, that provides value to an individual producer.

Besides the scientific aspect of marijuana production, patent protection is also challenging because the laws do not contain the same prohibitions as trademark law—immoral, deceptive, or scandalous. Presumably, the USPTO could grant a plant patent for newly invented or discovered marijuana plants, but so far this remains a gray area of the law.

There are pending marijuana patent applications but it may be years before any decision is made. Alternatively, there are opportunities for patents on ancillary inventions, or those that have an application outside the scope of marijuana.

A perfect example is packaging. Some people have developed unique packaging systems to protect the flower, while other designs allow consumers to smell the product prior to purchase—sniff jar. So long as it can be shown that there is a non-marijuana use, the USPTO should be open to granting patent protection.

On to trademarks, that is, branding or good will. It is to let consumers know that if you go and buy a product, regardless of where you buy them, they are all going to be of the same quality. And it is important to understand that this does not mean the best quality or even good quality, just the same quality. Trademarks are designed to help consumers and prevent confusion, so consistency is key.

It is important to distinguish trademarks from patents. You have to obtain the patent thereby creating a race to create an invention and get the patent. It is to protect a person if they have invested money, research and development, things like that, to protect their rights associated with it. Trademarks, on the other hand, do not actually require you to have a registered trademark to establish protection. Use in commerce is the only requirement.

If you are selling your product, you have established use and someone else is not going to be able to register the mark. However, to prevent extra costs associated with enforcing your trademark, it is suggested you register your trademark at the state level. As previously mentioned, protection is not currently available at the federal level.

There is one additional IP topic that is worth discussing, but often gets overlooked: trade secrets. Trade secrets may be one of the most applicable areas of law to the marijuana industry as it protects information. Often this includes unpatented inventions, formulas and recipes, techniques, processes, marketing information, customer lists, and other business information that gives an advantage to the company. Unlike trademark and patent protection, which generally require registration, trade secrets are typically protected by non-disclosure agreements and internal company procedures.

The application of trade secret law to the marijuana industry should be readily apparent. Many of the procedures and processes cannot be protected under patent law or patent law is inapplicable. In such instances, protecting a secret recipe or method for growing and cultivating marijuana is what sets one company apart from another. Moreover, because the various strains are available to all producers, it is these trade secrets that allow a company to distinguish its product from the competition. Who can grow the most pure product?

It might be the combination of humidity levels, ambient humidity in a controlled environment combined with the amount of light—how many lumens the plants are exposed to—with the combination of the particular fertilizer used. Additionally, there is the growing timeline, which includes the point at which the flowers are harvested, the method used for drying, the pesticides used, or lack thereof. All of these processes, individually or in combination, may be protected as a trade secret.

The one exception is information that is generally known as common knowledge in the industry. The Coca-Cola recipe may be the best and most widely known example of a trade secret. Many companies have their own cola, but there is only one Coca-Cola.

Because trade secrets are primarily regulated internally—based on business procedures and non-disclosure agreements—remedies for misappropriation are limited to injunctions, which prevents others from using a trade secret that was unlawfully obtained and financial compensation for any losses attributed to the theft or profits acquired by the thief. Any injunction will likely continue until such point the trade secret is no longer a secret.

Given the nature of the marijuana industry as an agricultural product where research and design is constantly occurring, it is important to understand that the trade secret law does not protect a company if someone independently develops the same product or processes. This emphasizes the importance of trademark protection and the interweaving nature of intellectual property rights. There is tremendous value in a proprietary trade secret, but only to the extent that consumers are familiar with the product they are receiving. Do consumers recognize the brand as a top-shelf product?

Personality rights are a quickly developing area with regard to marijuana. In just the past couple months, celebrities and their estates have been aligning their names with various marijuana products and prior to legalization, strains were named after celebrities who had a following in the marijuana industry (e.g. Snoop's Dream). At this point, it is unclear whether Snoop Dogg himself could bring a claim for misappropriation. In many instances, there is the issue of waiver that would prevent someone from bringing a claim for something they knew existed.

If a person is aware their personality rights are being misappropriated but fail to enforce those rights, the court can find they can waive any claim. However, given that marijuana has been illegal until 2012 in every state and is still federally illegal, a court may determine that one could not have enforced their personality rights and therefore the claim was not waived.

Tolling, or how long it has been out in the marketplace, is usually one of the most significant factors in determining whether misappropriation has occurred. Did a person take proactive steps to try and protect their rights or their personality associated with the product? Snoop's Dream has been around now for roughly five or six years as a strain. However, if there was no legal way for a person to enforce their rights or personality or name associated with it until now, have their rights been preserved?

CONSUMER PROTECTION

The challenges with IP laws and Personality Rights also present the issue of consumer protection. Currently, there are no standardization measures. Anyone can grow a particular strain and there is little protection for the consumer.

There is no assurance they will get the same product when purchased from multiple producers. Thereby further emphasizing the importance of the trademark. Rather than simply having Snoop's Dream it will need to be further designated by the producer's mark, for instance, "Avitas' Snoop's Dream."

Marijuana strains can be broken down into three common categories: sativa, indica, and hybrid (sativa-indica blend). Producers are required to submit samples for quality assurance testing, but this is not for the purpose of identifying to the customer what product they are receiving. Rather, it is more about determining the potency of the marijuana. Consider the following scenario: if Snoop's Dream is a hybrid that a producer sells, but somebody else labels their product as Snoop's Dream and its pure indica, you're getting a totally different product that has a totally different effect on the body.

There is nothing in place right now to protect this from occurring, but this is also a big argument for the continued legalization of marijuana. Whether or not consumer protections will be provided by the state or federal government remains in question. At this point, it seems more likely that the industry will provide its own protection and regulations to protect its own interests. For instance, an industry regulatory body may emerge and stamp products that meet industry standards as "industry approved" or with the name of the particular regulatory body.

Understanding the importance of business and marketing is what separates the high-end producer/processors from the amateur people who, frankly, I don't think are going to make it. You're not just growing weed. It is a business and part of running a business is ensuring that you have inventory that you can provide to your retailers on a regular basis.

part four

VOTER INITIATIVE

STATE LAW ON CONTROLLED SUBSTANCES

At the state level, most states have adopted versions of Uniform Controlled Substances Act. For instance, RCW 69.50 is Washington's Uniform Controlled Substances Act, which formalizes I-502 and provides regulations regarding the enforcement, production, and distribution of marijuana.

The trend of marijuana in Washington is very much in flux. There are issues with the number of medical marijuana dispensaries and the lack of regulation and how symbiosis can be created with the recreational industry. We speculate that the medical marijuana industry will be rolled into the recreational industry. The city of Tacoma has basically said it's an access issue. What they're using it for, whether it's for medicinal or recreational, ultimately doesn't matter.

Does a person have the ability to get access to it? If we're providing access through recreational production and sale, we don't need to provide access through medical. What remains unknown, and will be an interesting topic in this year's legislative session, is how the state plans to address the existing medical marijuana dispensaries. Anyone who has driven through the greater Seattle area has likely seen the green crosses, which represent a medical marijuana dispensary.

The question is whether they convert those over to recreational or shut them down. I would hope they do not convert them over to recreational because of all the hoops our clients have had to deal with in getting a recreational marijuana business up and running with all the regulations and all the fees they've had to pay.

The license lottery, created a mad panic where all these people had to submit their name in hopes of getting a state license to produce, if your name wasn't called, you were not legally in the marijuana business. Then all of a sudden you're going to give all these medical dispensaries out to anyone with an outstretched hand. Specifically, what I am saying is that if you wanted to get a producer/processor or retail license, you submitted an application, and then your application was subject to a lottery system.

There is also speculation that the federal government could reschedule marijuana so it could be removed from Schedule I and listed under Schedule II or III, or possibly removed from the lists altogether. By removing it from Schedule I, it would mean that there'd be more options to use it and more industries would be accessible. There would be an ambulatory structure. If people in the industry wanted to try to get something changed immediately, rescheduling may be where they want to focus. Alternatively, the federal government could recognize state laws—they wouldn't reschedule it, but create an exception for state laws.

This means that there would no longer be a federal enforcement against the use of it, even if it were still illegal in other states.

Many different people were discussing different ways marijuana would be addressed federally and it was not speculated that the budget would prohibit funds from being used towards prosecution of people operating legally under state regulations. This was not at the top of the list of people's speculations for the route the federal government was going to take, and so this was a little unexpected.

This is because ultimately the budget approach doesn't address many of the problems. It provides some peace of mind, but with it still being Schedule I, the federal issues are still an issue. It's a sound gradual step and a great way for the federal government to show its stance.

The removal of marijuana from the Uniformed Controlled Substances Act is another stance that people think could happen. The problem is the political headache it creates across the country because there are only four states that have legalized marijuana at this point. What happens to the other 46? Do you undermine state law by changing the federal treatment of it? It's an undecided question.

The best solution if you wanted something very soon might be to try to lobby for federal recognition of state laws. There are a lot of resources out there dealing with the federal level, because the federal law is omnipresent in every state.

Let's move back to state laws because this is a book about Washington State marijuana laws under I-502. It's important to have a backdrop understanding of the federal stance, but there are other resources on the topic. In Washington State, they have divided the industry from the seed to consumer consumption into three parts: producers, processors, and retailers.

The producers are the people who are planting the seeds and growing and harvesting the plants. The processors are the people who package the usable marijuana and sell it to retailers. The retailers are the storefronts where consumers select which product to purchase.

In other business models this may more traditionally be referred to as the producers, wholesalers, and retailers.

The primary difference being that the wholesaler would have purchased the branded product. In this instance, the processor is taking it from the raw product through to the wholesale product. The I-502 industry has more closely integrated more of the processing than that of more traditional industries. Juxtaposition, Oregon has four levels: producer, processor, wholesaler, and retailer. And Oregon allows for vertical integration. Vertical integration is where many components from seed to retailer are operated under one business entity.

Back to Washington, which, after understanding the producer, processor, retailer divisions, the next most significant part of Washington's structure is that they've drawn a line between the producer/processor side and the retailer side. Washington, at this point, bars vertical integration from the seed to consumer sale. If you're a producer or processor, you cannot also be a retailer. Further, a producer/processor can't have any financial interest in a retailer.

Alternatively, you can be on both the producer and processor license, so long as it remains a single entity. Now there's also a degree of horizontal integration. You can have your name on only one producer/processor license, or three retail licenses within jurisdictional requirements. The jurisdictional requirements are that you cannot have more than thirty-three percent of the retail licenses in any one jurisdiction, which may be either a county or city.

This is very complex because when we think jurisdictions as attorneys, we usually think a specific city, county, state, or federal jurisdiction. However, jurisdiction for these retail licenses and the thirty-three percent requirement is based upon the initial allocation of retail licenses—from the very beginning when they did the license lottery and designated where they wanted to have retail stores.

The thing with the jurisdiction is that some cities opted to choose whether or not they wanted to have licenses allocated for their city, or be part of the county as a whole. For example, King County is really populous with a lot of larger and smaller cities based on population. In designating the jurisdictions for licensees, there's King County at large, which are licenses that can go anywhere in King County except in cities, for example, Renton and Seattle, that opted to have their own lottery.

If the city of Renton said, "We are going to allow five licenses in Renton," then somebody who received a King County at large license would be prohibited from operating inside of Renton. That's why jurisdiction is complex, because you have to actually look at the specific license a person has and determine if it's the county at large or if it's the city, and once you figure that out, they can't have more than thirty-three percent of the licenses in the given jurisdiction.

Keep in mind this only applies to retailers—if producer/processor, you can only be on one—and the jurisdiction requirement is based on the allocation, or pending applications, not who's open for business. If one person is really quick and they have all their stuff together, they could be the only three open in a county.

Obviously, they would control one hundred percent of the jurisdiction. A producer, or the one who grows it, can go anywhere in the state when they get their one license and they can supply or sell it to any retailer who has a license anywhere in the state. They cannot, however, cross over into the medical side. You must stay dedicated to recreational usage.

This is an important point—producers who grow can only sell their product to processors and other producers. There is no intermediary. You couldn't set up a wholesaler and say, "I don't want to grow the stuff. I just want to be the middleman." You can't do that, because only people who have the licenses are allowed to sell. A huge part of this is the excise tax component. There's a twenty-five percent excise tax on every transaction relating to the marijuana.

If the producer sells its product to a separate processor, the twenty-five percent tax applies; the processor to the retailer would be taxed at twenty-five percent; and then the retailer to the customer is taxed at twenty-five percent, thereby making seventy-five percent of the consumer cost in state taxes.

However, there are two very, very important exceptions here. One is that if a producer and a processor license are owned by the same entity, they're exempt. Not every, but almost every producer also has a processor license.

In our experience, the people my office deals with are more on the business side. But a lot of times these are farmers who merely want to grow marijuana. They don't want to process or package their crops. They don't want to deal with the processing or wholesale side of the business. Consider that you don't find a lot of hops growers who also sell beer. They sell hops to Budweiser, who make the beer.

The second exception to the excise tax is processor-to-processor sales. The reason I really emphasize this is that this is perhaps one of the most significant exceptions affecting the market share race going on right now. You can actually transfer it to another entity without having the twenty-five percent tax, which is big. This provides just a sniff of where we believe the race to market share is really going to be, and who is going to be the first to big marijuana—who is going to emerge as the big brand?

One might ask: is this like developing co-ops, friendships, or franchises? Groups who've joined together to form some big thing? The problem is that one cannot have their name listed on more than one license. The question is how exactly can you do that; create such a model, and still remain compliant with the laws? There are two primary approaches that are emerging. One is a real estate oriented approach. The other is a processor-oriented approach.

Before digging further into these approaches, it is first important to understand some of the requirements imposed upon for each licensee. The current law does not provide any limit on the total number of licenses—instead, a statewide canopy size limitation was created. Canopy size does not refer to the size of the shaded veranda—it refers to the square footage of the floor space within which a licensee is allowed to grow marijuana plants.

If a single plant takes up 3 square feet, and you have ten plants; then you would need 30 square feet of approved canopy space. Let's tie this back around to the number of licenses the State ultimately decided to allow—the number of licenses directly relates to Washington's total statewide cap on the cumulative size of the canopy that will be allowed, currently 2 million square feet.

Since supply has been a problem, Washington State recently amended the canopy limitation to be 8.5 million square feet. However, the size of the canopy isn't the only factor that contributed to the supply issue. The difficulty in finding suitable legal locations for people to operate is arguably the bigger challenge.

I want to put a side note here for people not really familiar with the legal side of marijuana. There are three primary guiding areas of the law that you might want to be aware of when you're looking at something like the marijuana industry. One is I-502, the voter approved initiative that was then passed into statutory law. The Revised Code of Washington is the statutes, that's 69.50: Washington's Uniform Controlled Substances Act. Second is the administrative regulations. Those are the Washington Administrative Code (WACs). WACs are not voter initiatives that have been legislatively passed. They are passed by the regulating agency that's been charged with administering the statute. Third, judicial precedent or court cases may further refine the way the statutes and the regulations are interpreted.

What is important to understand is that a statute is something that is approved in a state either by the people through a vote or by the representatives in the legislature. At the regulatory level, the executive branch (the governor and the agencies under the governor) draft rules in accordance with the statutes. This is where the Liquor Control Board has a committee of five people who draft a way to interpret and implement the statute.

This administrative process is where the two million square foot canopy is established—this includes very rigid requirements, such as providing for the opportunity for public opinion, public comment, and redrafting. It took over a year for the LCB to complete this process. It is by way of the administrative code that applications were only accepted during a thirty day window. As of right now, there are no more applications being accepted and no more pending licenses being issued.

In discussing the canopy limitations, the reason it is really important to clarify the source of law is that it is much more difficult to change a statute because you have to have the consent of the people or their representatives. Whereas administrative interpretation or administrative implementation is easier, because you only go through a public noticing period where you allow people to see what you propose and you accept comments. Comments which are not binding, and only need be accepted by the agency.

Let's further divide regulations into two parts: (1) actual regulations and (2) temporary rules. Temporary or emergency rules can be enacted immediately, which has been an issue in counties and cities. For example, cities and counties can immediately pass what they call emergency or temporary moratoriums, banning all I-502 related operations. These can be enacted without notice and without public comments. The emergency moratorium may last thirty to ninety days, at which point the governing authority could have drafted and voted on permanent regulations, which would make the moratorium ban permanent.

The LCB implemented the statewide canopy limitation. They originally thought two million would provide for enough marijuana, but the proposal to increase the canopy to 8.5 million square feet suggests otherwise. The importance of the Cole Memo with regard to this is huge. That two million expected to be specifically how much they thought the state needed. The reason they had to be so conservative with that number is to keep the federal government out of the picture.

If they followed Colorado's lead, there would be more risk of diversion of product outside the state. The idea with the two million was that we needed to create the perfect number for exact consumption in Washington. Take for instance the beer industry—seventy-eight percent of the world's hops are grown in Washington State.

What the LCB wanted to prevent was seventy-eight percent of the world's marijuana being produced in the state of Washington. The LCB wanted one hundred percent of marijuana grown in Washington consumed in Washington—zero percent going anywhere else. A way to do that, at least to start, was to put a square foot canopy limitation on how much marijuana could be grown.

Besides the statewide canopy, the LCB further broke the producer side into three different tiers. Tier 1 is the smallest and Tier 3 is the largest. A Tier 3 producer can grow 10,000 to 30,000 square feet, Tier 2 can grow 2,000 to 10,000 square feet, and Tier 1 can grow less than 2,000 square feet. To further show the federal government that the state is serious about keeping marijuana within our state borders, the LCB retained the right to limit how much individual growers produce.

Temporary regulations are currently in place limiting capacity by thirty percent. Instead of having a 30,000 square foot canopy, a Tier 3 producer can only have 21,000 square feet.

A common question is why the state is increasing the overall canopy to 8.5 million square feet if they're not even allowing them to use the full 2 million? We don't know if they might issue more licenses for growers or if they're going to expand the capacity of the existing growers. You would think that they'd want to expand the existing ones because they're already up in place and, presumably, operating.

For producers, this two million canopy was used to determine the number of total licenses allowed. The number of retailers was determined by a joint effort of the LCB and Office of Financial Management, taking into account population, security and safety issues, and discouraging illegal markets. A lottery system was used to determine who would be granted a retail license and to limit the number of retail stores per county.

The LCB chose a lottery system as the most fair and equitable system for issuing licenses where there were more applications than the number of licenses allotted.

Now we've talked about the licenses, and that was the key thing, to decide how it was legally going to be produced, distributed, and retailed. Now, what are the requirements to be a licensee? This is a common question we receive from potential clients—they want to know what it means to be a resident. Most of these requirements arc statutory. One, you must be a Washington resident. That's one of the biggest requirements.

Oregon's Measure 91, which was just passed, does not have that same requirement—subject to change based on the Oregon Liquor Control Commission's rulemaking. In Washington, you've got to be a resident for at least ninety days to qualify for a license. Even if you moved here for no other reason than to have your name on a license, it's fine so long as you have been a resident for ninety days.

At this point in time, most people are approaching the residency requirement from the perspective of the Department of Revenue. The Department of Revenue in Washington has a very specific definition they apply to who they treat as a resident for taxation purposes. The issue is that this definition is pretty broad because, of course, Washington State wants to sweep as many people as possible into the residency definition for revenue and taxation purposes. However, it wasn't necessarily intended to have that same level of broadness in defining what residency meant for purposes of an I-502 licensee.

However, the definition under that includes anything from voter registration, to obtaining a driver's license, to your primary place of residence. If you're a registered voter in the state of Washington, you're a resident. If you have a primary residence in Washington, a place that you live, you're a resident. What becomes the more difficult question is when must your ninety-day residency be established? This is certainly a gray area due to differing information being provided by the LCB.

To clarify the question, when must a true party of interest or financier need to have met the ninety-day residency requirement? At the time the application was submitted or at the time of the lottery? At the time that the LCB is conducting the initial interview? From the date of the final issue of the license? From the date that you start operations?

The answer is in typical lawyer fashion, it depends, which may not even be adequate due to the differing information available.

There are three key points that I think everyone thinks about with regard to the residency requirement. There was ninety days before the initial pending license was granted, before you even won the lottery. There is ninety days before the submission of a change of membership form is processed. And there is ninety days before the final license was issued.

Let's consider the following hypothetical: the application for the license was submitted on December 1, 2013 and you were a Washington State resident as of June 1, 2013. You would have met the ninety-day residency requirement. Conversely, what if the license was submitted on December 30, 2013 and you were not a resident until October 1, 2013? Was it the day that the window was closed or is it the date of the lottery?

If you became a resident on December 1, 2013, submitted the application on December 2, but the lottery wasn't held so you didn't even know if you were getting into the process until June. The lottery was actually held much quicker, but the issue is still relevant.

The current pressing question is the residency timeline for new investors. Consider a company that is in need of additional capital and you want to become an investor, but you are not a resident of Washington State. Immediately you have to begin the process of becoming a resident and then have that ninety-day window. Once again, when must the ninety-day residency be established? The question is ninety-days before what? Is it before you submit a change of membership form to add you as an owner?

It should also be clarified that a license held in the name of a business entity does not circumvent the residency requirements. As will be further discussed, any true party of interest, which includes LLC members and corporate stockholders, must meet the residency requirements. They cannot hide behind the business entity or corporation.

With regard to the typical licensee, most licenses are held in the name of an entity. As a matter of fact, licenses that are held by an individual are allowed, by the LCB, to form an entity and move the license into it. Once that's done—this is moving more into the legal principle side—that license can never change names to another entity or back to the individual. It's important to note that all entities must be a recognized Washington State entity.

The license is not, from a legal perspective, considered property. It is permission to do something—a license to produce, process, or sell marijuana. Even though that permission has a real, monetized value, it's not something you can transfer from one person to the next. They are so aptly named "non-transferable licenses."

Consider the following: say you are a producer and you are not using your processor license. You may want to get rid of it, but you cannot sell it or split it off to another entity. It's a double edged sword. You get around the previously mentioned excise tax issue, but nobody may end up using it. However, it's important to know the LCB has adopted the position, at this point, that you can split locations.

Because of the difficulty and the obstacles people have found in finding a suitable location for a producer/processor operation, you may have your producer in Eastern Washington and you may have your processor in Western Washington. They may be divided in separate places but still operate under the same Universal Business Identifier (UBI) assigned to each business entity, which is recognized by the state of Washington.

Moving a little deeper into who may obtain an I-502 license, there are two categories: financiers and true parties of interest. Anybody who meets the definition of being a true party of interest or a financier has to meet the requirements laid out by the LCB: (1) residency, (2) criminal background check, and (3) financial history. A true party of interest includes anyone with any sort of equity interest, even if they have merely a half percent. If it's a company or investment portfolio that has equity interest, then you look into that company or group of investors.

INTOXICATION: CRIME & PUNISHMENT

In many ways, public health and safety is the most omnipresent concern over legal marijuana—and nowhere has that concern been clearer than issues of intoxicated operation of a motor vehicle. Considerable time and resources were spent in carefully drafting this part of the law. Adopting these laws into the larger regime of law introduced strict enforcement and serious penalties.

Washington's recreational marijuana law chose THC as the psychoactive chemical for the purpose of standardizing the physical presence of an intoxicating substance in a person's body. The impairing effects caused by alcohol intoxication were used as the baseline to establish a similar impairment through THC intoxication. The existing limit of 0.08 blood alcohol concentration establishing the legal threshold for intoxication was approximated for an equivalent limit of five nanograms per milliliter of blood concentration for THC.

By law, the legal definition for intoxication in Washington is now five nanograms per milliliter of THC or a 0.08 blood alcohol. However, unlike tests for blood alcohol level, no such test yet exists for the measure of a person's THC level. The only method for reliable measurement is to draw and test a person's blood—a method for which no field sobriety test exists.

At present, the accepted current standard is probable cause as determined by an officer, upon which the officer may compel and accompany such a person to the police station for the purpose to draw a blood sample.

This is a very interesting area where you're dealing with laws regarding DNA and body fluids. The approach has been that you can be forced to give blood and if you refuse, it could be a presumption that you are going to have to overcome. The LCB says it can take up to three hours in some people after one serving to reach the five nanogram per milliliter level.

It can take longer depending on a bunch of factors, such as gender, body size, and the like. Current guidance under the laws is to wait five hours after consumption before operating a vehicle. Edibles carry the risk of maiming your system longer because of the digestion process.

Other legal requirements in Washington are the age limit—only adults over the age of twenty-one can purchase or possess marijuana and a valid ID is required. This restriction includes being on the retail premises. Another important regulation is that marijuana can only be sold and purchased at state-licensed retail stores and must be consumed within the state of Washington, but only on private property.

Cash-handling and traditional transaction methods presents yet another challenge. There are a lot of retail marijuana stores that only accept cash and this has to do with banking and credit card restrictions. Most credit card companies expressly prohibit the use of credit card transactions for any federally prohibited purchase or sale, and that includes marijuana.

This also extends to the use of ATM machines within the building. Early on, people were putting ATMs in their retail locations as a way to offset the inconvenience of not allowing the use of credit cards. ATM companies have followed the lead of the credit card companies and now prohibit their use in marijuana retail stores.

The next limitation is the purchasing limits. Adults over twenty-one can purchase up to one ounce of usable marijuana, which is the harvested flower or the bud, up to sixteen ounces of marijuana-infused edibles in solid form, seventy-two ounces in liquid form, and up to seven grams of marijuana concentrates.

There are no resell or giveaways allowed under Washington law for recreational marijuana use. It is a felony for anyone but a licensed retailer to sell or provide marijuana to anyone else. Providing or selling marijuana to a minor under the age of eighteen is subject to ten years imprisonment and a $10,000 fine.

Obviously the most important provision is prohibition of selling to somebody else. One of the big issues that has been out there are delivery services. A quick search of Craigslist reveals a number of delivery options—all of which are illegal. It is also not difficult to find marijuana for sale. If you purchase any marijuana through any of those outlets, you are committing a crime.

For right now, purchase the marijuana yourself; there is no method for obtaining it otherwise. It has been proposed and speculated that there will likely be some other method or means for delivery discussed in the current legislative session.

One point worth clarifying is that you are not likely to encounter any kind of legal issue in the privacy of your own home—assuming that you are not violating some other law, meaning there is no justifiable reason for law enforcement to be involved or you are using in public view. However, it is always important to exercise a high degree of personal judgment in a situation such as this.

STATE LINES

We are advising clients right now that if you are an I-502 company in the State of Washington, you should not cross state lines with any part of your business. This is to avoid any potential challenges and includes any revenue associated with your business.

What that means is that if you are a producer/processor entity in the state of Washington, do not run the risk of thinking that merely because you have segregated operations in the state of Oregon under the same business entity that you are going to avoid any kind of prosecution. You are low-hanging fruit and easy to target.

A better approach is to completely separate out your business and form a new entity—a new operation. One of the approaches we recommend is the IP approach or market share approach. The idea is you have your business in Washington and a separate business in Oregon. So long as the entities are separate, you can own both of them.

What I would advise a client not to do is send fertilizer between the entities. Product is the most obvious example—you cannot produce marijuana in Washington and send it to Oregon for retail sales.

You really want to make sure to consult an attorney or a tax expert on this, making sure you have arm's length transactions, and you're complying with all transfer pricing requirements if you are crossing any kind of state or international border, to avoid even the appearance of violation via crossing state lines.

The Commerce Clause, which is beyond the scope of this book, certainly comes in here. Consult a professional attorney if you are considering doing any kind of interstate operations.

INDUSTRY INSIGHT:
EIGHT BALL

Craig Fitzgerald, OWNER
The Root Cellar, Retail Store

1. Chicken and the Egg

Sometimes the LCB leans on the license applicants to decide how to proceed in a new industry—meanwhile, 90% of the applicants have no idea what the business entails, so they're leaning on the LCB. At times it feels like you're standing there staring at the LCB while they just stand there staring right back.

2. Super-Special Pricing

Most licensees have discovered that premium prices are associated with all things related to the marijuana industry—services, products, etc. As soon as they find out you're involved in this industry, you find out they have a special marijuana price for everything. Honestly, it feels like extortion.

3. Marco? Polo!

Finding a suitable location can feel like 'whack-a-mole'—it's that simple. The LCB is great at eliminating sites, but it's up to the applicant to come up with an alternative when that happens.

4. The Dream Team

Know the people you're teaming up with—be sure to know the people you're getting in bed with. An investor may bring a bag of money, but it won't do you any good if they start throwing up hurdles to progress. This is just sound business advice, but goes triple in this industry.

5. Tick-Tock Times Three

Timing—take your best time estimate for everything and multiply by three. If you're lucky, that'll put you in the ballpark.

6. Jumping Ship

Optimism is essential, but blind-optimism gets people into trouble. Not everybody who quit well-paying professional careers stopped to weigh all of the potential repercussions if it takes longer than expected to get to first revenue.

7. Different Name, Same Game

The recreational marijuana industry is new—running a business is not. It requires effort, planning, adaptability, and yes, marketing. There are strict rules that govern some aspects of running the business due to the unique laws for recreational marijuana, but it still needs to be run like a business. The early days of standing in the river and having a fish jump into your arms are over, but the savvy business owners are still thriving. Fortunately, the margins have been pretty forgiving, so course corrections are an option. Eventually though, I think the competition is probably going to get fiercer.

8. Trolls

It might sound trivial, but, buy your domain name before licensing your business—seriously. There are foreign and domestic trolls who are scooping up domain names based on the LCB and Washington State business records. Who wants to pay $20/month just to use a domain that might otherwise have cost $12 or less for a whole year?

part five

Liquor Control Board

I-502: BROUGHT TO YOU BY THE LCB

Working with the Liquor Control Board

The Washington State Liquor Control Board ("LCB") can be your best friend. At the same time, you always have to take a lot of what you hear with a grain of salt.

I have hung up the phone on multiple occasions wondering whether I received reliable information from them. That is where the importance of working with an attorney comes in. You will need help to determine whether or not you could really rely on something that the LCB has told you or if you need to do a little more digging or call up and reconfirm what you were just told.

Like us—navigating this new area of the law—the LCB is also brand new to marijuana enforcement and regulation. It is important to understand some of the forces that are driving all of the individuals in this. As a government employee, licensing agent or otherwise, their primary concern is ensuring that they are operating conservatively and well within the rules. And so it is not in your interest to extend beyond that to try to find a way to navigate beyond an area of uncertainty.

But what they will try to do is help you, and make sure you are in compliance, which is a much better approach than finding out after the fact. There is the axiom, "Sometimes it's better to ask forgiveness than permission."

This is not one of those times. This is an instance where it is much better, safer and less expensive, in most cases, to ask permission rather than forgiveness, because ultimately the risk is forfeiture or having to adapt to costly changes.

LICENSE SCARCITY

Currently, companies holding licenses and people listed on those licenses are allowed to be True Parties of Interest to a single company with one producer and up to one processor, or alternatively, up to three retail licenses. Additional limits have been placed on the size of marijuana grow operations and a licensee's ability to expand future operations, both of which restrict the capacity of I-502 companies sufficiently to curb any one company's ability to capture excessive market share at this time.

OUTCOME BY EXPECTATION?

Concern is rising among leaders in the industry that an LCB projection that half of licensees will fail is less an expectation from observation, and more like expectation for an outcome whose objective they have accepted. A core directive to the LCB is "ensuring the success of the industry." Conversely, the LCB is controlling the licenses available, who can work in the marijuana industry, and where these licenses may be located. Is it not their intent to ensure the industry is successful? What is the point of a limitation on licenses?

COMMUNICATION WITH THE LIQUOR CONTROL BOARD

At some point, in most cases several months later, there's the day that the LCB calls up out of the blue and says they are ready to start moving you through the process—this is the initial conversation. A more formal initial interview will be scheduled at a later date. This conversation signifies that an LCB agent (or investigator) has been assigned to the license, and he or she will work with the licensee for the remainder of the licensing process.

The LCB has approximately 15 agents. They initially started with just a few, which is part of the reason the backlog was so severe for a while. Currently, they are up to speed and moving people through a lot quicker.

From that initial conversation, you're looking at an indeterminate length of time based on various factors moving through the licensing process. In most cases, if an individual was a resident ninety days before the initial conversation, they're pretty much OK. That is moving into the grayer area because it's not as clear of a distinction between ninety days before the application was submitted, or ninety days between winning the license lottery and the initial interview.

Residency is such a huge issue because there are a lot of people who are outside Washington trying to get involved. For example, there are a lot of people who have been very successful in the medical marijuana industry in other states. They see the trend in the industry nationwide is probably going to shift toward recreational. They're anxious to get a foot in the door and be one of the first to transition over to Washington State. Many of these people are used to the Commerce Clause and the fact that they can do business all over the state and here, in Washington, you can't do that. It's a whole different environment.

The Commerce Clause is from the Constitution and says the federal government will have authority to pass laws relating to any commerce that is crossing state lines, because it becomes federal commerce at that point. In order to avoid that toehold into regulating Washington's marijuana industry, the state of Washington has said we're going to keep this commerce, this industry, solely within the Washington State borders. Even if it's legal in Oregon, we're not going to allow it to cross that border. We're not going to give the federal government the Commerce Clause tie-in to step in and do anything.

The residency requirement also becomes an issue related to the Commerce Clause. If you're a resident of Washington, your dollars should be Washington dollars, so you're not moving funds, say for investment purposes, across state lines. The bottom line is any investor in this industry, has to look at an investor pool that's inside Washington. You have to look at a director and officer pool that's already inside Washington. You can't pull somebody from another state who is a business expert and bring him or her in, at least during the initial process.

The criminal background check is another qualification for any financier or true party of interest. The code (WAC 314-55-040) is pretty self-explanatory and uses a point system where different violations are scored based on severity. Any applicant that has accumulated more than eight points will normally be denied a license.

To put that into perspective, a felony conviction that occurred during the previous ten years is assigned twelve points and misdemeanors in the past three years may be either four or five points each. Failure to disclose any criminal history is an automatic four points, thereby making two non-disclosures a likely denial of the license.

Non-disclosure relates to any prior criminal history, regardless of whether or not points would be assigned. For instance, someone with a felony from eleven years ago would not be assigned points if properly disclosed—due to exceeding the ten year window—but failure to disclose would incur the four point penalty.

One common question, is whether there are any exceptions for marijuana-related offenses, because inevitably you're going to get people with marijuana related violations in their past. The LCB has stated that any single state or

federal conviction for the growing, possession, or sale of marijuana will be considered
for mitigation on an individual basis.

Mitigation will be considered based on the
quantity of product involved and other circumstances surrounding the conviction. It's
worth noting that part of the reason they are
legalizing marijuana is because they're trying
to force it out of the black market.

STRATEGIC TRANSPARENCY

One strategy that an individual might want to
consider in the course of transparency and
communication with neighbors is to offer
some facts that may reassure the neighbors as
to the security. The fact of the matter is that
this is not some unsupervised outdoor garden
where anybody can walk in and harvest their
own weed. This is not where you are going to
see people visiting and smoking weed on the
front porch.

You are dealing with a location where consumption or use of marijuana is going to be
strictly prohibited and regulated because employees cannot be intoxicated when they are

on the property. You cannot extend invitations for the public to come in and sample the product. The public may arrange tours, but use of marijuana on the property is absolutely prohibited.

DISCLOSURES

Quite possibly the most important aspect in dealing with the Liquor Control Board (LCB) is disclosure and transparency.

We have so many clients who come to us and say, "Yeah, I want to bring you in as an attorney. I need some advice on this and we need assistance." It turns out that the reason they are seeking an attorney and want advice is because they failed to disclose something to the LCB. They weren't transparent with the LCB and now the LCB may have requested specific or additional business documentation which may not be available or the client may have failed to disclose a felony to the LCB. Our clients want to know, "how do I handle this?" or "we're about to do this deal. We're getting the money. Can I do this and circumvent the rule?"

I think that there's a prevalent attitude among people who are entering in the marijuana industry, particularly among those who have been operating in the black market, to be suspicious of any government authority. Such people often worry that all of these LCB investigations are really about trapping those involved in the industry. This is not the case.

As an attorney, one of the first things I tell a new client is, "look, the LCB is looking at how they can get you through the process. They're not looking at how they can prevent you from getting through the process." Without variation, my experience shows that people who disclose information and are transparent with the LCB, find that the LCB is willing to help them work through the process.

They're trying to find ways that you can meet their requirements and still move through it. The LCB understands the challenges with this process and so when you are disclosing things that might be problematic to you, they see it as, "all right, they've come up against this challenge." The LCB ultimately has discretion and a lot of deadlines are put in place, which can be extended when necessary.

For instance, there is a common six-month window that can be used as both an extension and penalty, depending on the situation. It's an automatic ding in most cases where an applicant fails to follow LCB procedures in adding new investors or merely keeping the LCB informed regarding certain structural changes. Alternatively, it may be viewed as an extension where an applicant is having challenges locating a suitable property, but expresses to the LCB its continued desire to operate under the license.

Consider the following scenario: We have people who come to us and say, "OK, I know that I'm going to be subject to a six-month wait period because of this thing that I'm facing right now, and oh by the way I may not have told the LCB that I was going to be facing this, and now it's happened. I was hoping that it wouldn't. What do I do?"

You wait six months and see what happens.

If you're not ready to go at the initial interview, a better situation would be to wait until you are sufficiently prepared. There is an assumption based off of initial indications from the LCB that if you weren't ready to go and start moving through the process at the moment of the initial interview, you are going to automatically be subject to a six-month wait period.

When the LCB calls for the initial interview, it is acceptable to tell them you are still getting things in order and to request additional time. My experience has been that they are willing to accept such requests for a reasonable amount of time and with reasonable justification.

Part of that may be attributed to, as a firm, having a positive reputation with the LCB. They know who we are and have worked with us before. If we're helping facilitate that licensing process, the LCB is more likely to say, "OK, yeah, we know that you're going to come to us, the LCB, and check in with us. You're making our life easier. We love that. Great. Let us know when you get everything lined up. That's fine."

If on the other hand the LCB calls you up and they say, "All right, initial conversation time," and you say, "Yeah, this is where our location is going to be, blah, blah, blah." A month later you realize, "Ah, dang, that letter of intent didn't materialize into a purchase or sale of the property. I have to now go to this other location." Now you're going to tell the investigator, "By the way, our site is now changing to this other one." Boom, the six-month wait period.

That is an example of where you need to be transparent with the LCB. If it's a site that you think you're going into but you haven't completed the transaction, don't tell them that you have secured that site.

If it's a site that you think you're going into but you haven't received approval from the port yet, don't tell them that you're definitely going to go into that site and fail to disclose the fact that you still are subject to approval by the port. Disclose the fact that you're still subject to getting your business licenses approved by a local city or the county.

That way, when the county says, "Yeah, we're now passing this moratorium so anybody who hasn't received their license yet, you're no longer going to be approved. You're not going to be able to be licensed and processed." The LCB is going to say; "Why the hell did you tell us you got your business licenses when you were still a week or two out from getting your zoning approval?"

Now that the moratorium has been passed, you've got to start over and the LCB is going to apply the six-month hold. If on the other hand, you've been transparent with them and honest from the beginning, then the LCB is willing to work with you.

While not getting the six-month ding is hugely important when you are locking down a property, in other instances when you haven't made any progress at all it's helpful. You can tell them that you are looking at this property, and it fell through. We're still trying and being upfront. You're not trying to impress the LCB. You don't want to tell them that you are further along than you are. They don't care, they just want to know what is going on.

Keeping them in the loop and showing that you are actively working on it is going to keep them from dropping you altogether, which they certainly can do if you give any timeline but don't meet it.

To be clear, the LCB can withdraw your license and the only remedy you would have is to pursue a different license. Keeping in mind that the LCB is no longer issuing licenses, which means licenses are only available on the secondary market—taking or purchasing an interest.

There are people who, at first blush, might appear to be true parties of interest, but who aren't because they fall into some of the few exceptions that apply. Typically, this is somebody with a certain amount of control over the business operations, but does not actually make business decisions. We have had a lot of discussions about what it means to control the business, as it is a very fine line.

For example, the master grower may seem, initially, as having control over the business because he is the one that oversees the entire growing operation. He has the timelines, oversees all the staff who harvest and trim the plants, but that is not considered "control over the business." That is control over the operation. He can't control the finances. He can't direct all the different components of the costs, the dividends, or to whom they are selling.

He's not controlling the business operations itself, merely a process that's a component of the business. Therefore, he's not a true party of interest merely by virtue of the fact that he's participating in the operations. Employ-ees, basic worker bees, are also not true parties of interests. However, if an employee is given an ownership interest, that throws a wrench into all this.

Let's consider some of the big picture things the LCB is going to consider when determin-ing who is a true party of interest. Aside from control, the LCB is going to consider whether you own part of the company. If you are not an owner, the LCB will consider whether you are you acting like an owner of the company. Is your compensation so tied to the profita-bility of the company that in essence you are an owner?

You might not technically be an owner, but this does not always insulate you from being considered a true party of interest. You can act like an owner, without being an owner, and still be considered a true party of interest. That is determined by looking at whether you are being paid a percentage of profits based on revenue.

Perhaps the biggest exception to who is con-sidered a true party of interest is a landlord or person who owns the property. They are not considered a true party of interest so long as the compensation for the property to the landlord is not directly tied to the profitability of the company.

We've already talked about how difficult it is to find this land. There's nothing to prevent a landlord from charging an exorbitant rate for the leasing of the land. They can charge $5,000, $6,000, $7,000 on what may ordinarily be a $2,000 or $3,000 piece of property, but because the uses are for marijuana, they can charge that premium rate.

In other industries, landlords will often base rent on profit or revenue. This is not allowed under I-502. You can't tie anything to revenue or profit.

Example Scenario 5.1

Consider the following example, which considers a typical lease arrangement in the restaurant industry:

Damon's Restaurant is going to operate on a piece of property located in the Jantzen Beach Mall Shopping Center on Hayden Island. The rent that Damon's restaurant is going to pay is structured into two parts. The initial base amount, which is $15,000, is paid each month no matter what. In addition to the base fee, if

Damon's revenue, or sales, exceeds a certain point, say $200,000 per month, they have to pay an additional five percent for the first $100,000 and four percent on the second $100,000. This would continue until it got down to two percent for anything thereon after. Each month, Damon's rent is dependent on total revenue.

In this scenario, the LCB would look at the Jantzen Beach Shopping Mall Center as a true party interest because they are being compensated in proportion to the gross sales.

Often times, someone who is investing in real estate does not want to be a true party of interest. There are numerous reasons, and it may be as simple as not wanting to be residents of Washington or they're not a current resident, thereby not meeting the ninety-day residency requirement. A lot of companies, such as investors in the Canadian marijuana market or US medical marijuana companies, want to invest in the recreational marijuana industry.

What they are doing is purchasing the property, then turning around and leasing it to recreational marijuana operations. They may not want to do that for a single piece of property, but they want to do it for a dozen pieces of property because they have $50 million or $100 million available to invest. They can only do that if they can avoid being a true party of interest.

If they were residents, even in the state of Washington, they would be limited to a single producer/processor operation because now they are going to be listed on the license as a true party interest. Whether or not they had actual ownership of the company, their compensation structure is such that they are going to be viewed as a true party of interest. To avoid that, rent or leasing expenses would have to be based on a flat amount each month that is not subject to how the business is doing.

One approach a portion of these groups are taking is placing a premium price on land that can be used for producing marijuana. At this point, to date, the premium rate has not been challenged under the exception that it is provided for in landlord real estate agreements because it is a fixed amount. That may change at any point and frankly, a lot of people speculated that it will be changed at some point because there's a threshold after which the question is, "Are you kind of acting like an owner here?"

To qualify this point, it is difficult to determine exactly how much the property is worth. Yes, there is increased risk of failure for the marijuana producer/processors as opposed to some other industries. The landlords are justified in raising the rates.

However, you cannot raise the rates so high that you are going to bankrupt the producer/processor. Finding that balance is difficult. That's why traditionally there's a component of the payment that will be structured as a net or gross component of proceeds.

An alternative approach in the real estate industry that is common to deal with has been to structure the compensation based on cash collected rather than on revenue. The Department of Revenue (IRS) has always treated this structure as not being a net gross structure, one that would fall under what the LCB is using to determine a true party of interest.

Under the cash-collected model, the payment made to the landlord may be tied to cash rather than revenue. However, the amount owed may be much higher, at an exorbitant rate.

Let's use $5 per square foot of land as an example. You are not really sure what a sustainable rent will be, but you estimate between $2 and $3 per square foot for the property. You do not want to bankrupt your tenant or business, so you initially opt for $2 per square foot per month. Two years down the road you anticipate being at $3 per square foot per month, if they're profitable. It's difficult to determine.

What people are considering, as is common in other industries, is setting the rate at $5 per square foot per month. That's what they owe under the terms of the lease. However, the tenant only pays on that $5 per square foot per month an amount owed based on the amount of cash as it is collected. Even though you may owe $50,000 this month in rent, if you only collected enough money to pay $20,000 per month, the remaining $30,000 would roll over to the next month. It has an accumulative effect toward the end of the lease.

This accumulated amount may eventually be written off, if the business fails, or forgiven at the end of the lease. It is important to note that we are solely dealing with the LCB and its definition of a true party of interest in describing this landlord/tenant lease approach. There are important tax implications—anyone interested in using such a model should talk with an attorney.

I also want to point out here that you may think that an under the table deal or a side handshake deal is going to save everybody a lot of hassle and alleviate the need to go through the LCB process—don't do this. It should not be expected that you are going to make a handshake deal—one that is not official—and avoid disclosure to the LCB.

It is for this same reason that I say the sooner you seek attorney services, the less money it is going to cost you in the end. Typically, if you come to us once the problem has arisen, you may pay two to three times the amount that it would have cost had you spoken with a lawyer right out of the gate.

The last point on this is the notion that audits are going to be common-place in this industry. It's going to exceed anything that is in any other industry, and businesses need to be disclosing everything. Do not deal with these under-the-table deals because how are you going to account for that extra, undocumented $100,000?

The real estate approach presents a lot of issues, and we are unsure if this will be the best long-term approach for outside investors, but it is likely a component of a successful market share.

THE REAL ESTATE INVESTMENT APPROACH

Cash collected is not tied to profit because the compensation is not a result of business judgment in the company. Anytime you've tied it to gross revenue or net proceeds, there's going to be some element of business judgment that determines how much you get, how profitable a business is and its net worth. How much revenue is generated is based on the business's operations and all of the aforementioned things.

But cash is about how much you operate. The only significance of cash, or what it's tied to, is how fast you have to pay the landlord. It doesn't determine the amount that's owed or the value of the purchase or possession rights of land. That amount is determined and fixed, unlike a net or gross agreement, which allows it to fluctuate, based on the business. Cash collected approach is a one hundred percent premature enterprise.

To expand on how the cash collected figure is determined; you never have to pay an amount that exceeds five percent of cash collected at the end of each month. The way that you're going to pay the landlord is $10,000 plus five percent of every dollar that comes through the door by the end of the month. It doesn't mean you still owe us a $100,000 each month, it means that you only have to pay us $10,000 plus 5% of the cash.

One of the exceptions to receiving compensation based on profits is that an employee can be compensated out of the profitability of the company or gross revenue of the company without being considered a true party of interest, so long as this compensation does not exceed twenty-five percent of their total salary. It has to be a structure or compensation that is typical, or not extraordinary in parallel to other industries or similar positions. The compensation can further be on the basis of overall profitability of the company, such as a bonus, but it must not be atypical.

This process whereby the LCB first makes a determination of who is a true party of interest or financier, that person is reported by the entity and needs to be qualified. One group that may be overlooked is the institutional investor/financier. All of the different people who invest into this portfolio that invests in a marijuana business will need to be qualified by the LCB. This is the reason that institutional investors have been almost entirely absent from the industry, except for a few rare instances in the past couple months.

There are too many risks, too many components for the company that could jeopardize their license and for a person who may or may not be aware that their money was being invested in marijuana. Considering financiers more broadly, a financier is someone interested in the marijuana industry, but not wanting the risk of being an owner.

FINANCIERS AS TRUE PARTIES OF INTEREST

A true party of interest is only permitted to invest in one producer license and one processor license, or up to three retail licenses—

all ownership further being subject to additional limitations. As with true parties of interest, anyone having an interest in a potential investment scenario, if meeting the financier definition, must likewise satisfy all individual qualification requirements, such as residency, criminal background check, and financial history/tracing.

These requirements are especially significant because of the restrictions extending all the way to anyone meeting the financier definition. Merely lending money to an I-502 company, such as to a family member, would then necessitate completion of all related, relevant LCB qualifications requirements. The underlying public policy for such treatment is driven largely to minimize the risk of federal interference.

A core concern is to deter the risk that the I-502 industry may provide financial subterfuge for laundering or similar activities of funds sourced from drug cartels or other organized criminal operations. All money used for the purpose of funding companies in the I-502 industry must provide clear evidence of acceptable funding sources and finances traceable to the satisfaction of the LCB's standards and in the discretion of the licensing agents conducting the appurtenant investigations.

FINANCIAL INVESTIGATIONS

Financial tracing is an interesting aspect of the Liquor Control Board investigation. First, they are going to investigate everybody contributing funds to the operation. A typical investigation starts with a review of the past six months of bank statements. This does not mean every account an individual has, but at the very least, any account that will be used to contribute to the company.

The LCB wants to know how much money you think it will take the start the company and where that money is coming from. For instance, if a person is worth $100 million, they will not need to give the LCB every account number for every dollar they have. However, if they estimate it will take one million dollars to start the company, the LCB will investigate where the one million dollars originates.

Note there is no significance to the million-dollar amount. That is a discretionary number. The LCB has not set a specific amount that they expect in capital for a person to have access to in starting the company. What they do not want and what they're looking for, in the discretion of the investigator, is whether the venture is sufficiently capitalized. For example, is it under-capitalized to the point that it's likely that they're going to turn to a source of funds that may not be qualified later in the process? Will the company need to turn to loan sharks or interested drug dealer for a $100,000 short-term loan to continue operations?

Beyond considering the estimated start-up capital, the LCB is also going to look at a 6-month history of your bank accounts. For example, if they see a $250,000 deposit, the LCB is going to ask you for the origination of those funds.

The significance of asking for six months in financial statements for the bank accounts you intend to use is to determine whether you may be misrepresenting or forthcoming about the source of those funds. Again, the purpose is to prevent illegal or out-of-state funds from investing in the company

Consider the following: You are a Washington resident with no money to invest, but through a handshake deal you are able to obtain $500,000 for your company. If you do not disclose the deal and you claim that this is your money to start the operation, the LCB is going to deny a license.

Furthermore, the LCB has the discretion to investigate further back than six months. They can ask for as much additional information as they want. However, this does not mean you will automatically be disqualified if $500,000 was dropped into your account. It may be an inheritance or other legitimate gift or investment. So long as there is a legitimate reason for a large deposit, unrelated to the I-502 business, the LCB is going to take no issue with the financial aspect of the business.

The bottom line is that this is an investigation and the LCB has discretion to determine the source of funds used for starting an I-502 company. Their intent is to prevent illegal or out-of-state funds from backing an operation, and not to prevent legitimate investors from moving forward. Much of dealing with the LCB feels like a black box, but most people are relieved when they understand it is mostly a procedural requirement and so long as you are upfront and transparent with the LCB, there are few issues you will run into.

SQUATTERS "GET OFF THE POT"

Squatters are people who applied for an I-502 license but have no intention of developing them—they are squatting on their rights. Squatters hold dozens of licenses throughout the state and do not care if they are subjected to a six-month waiting period each time the LCB calls. In our estimate there are two types of squatters. First, there are the existing medical marijuana operations. They oppose a retail location opening in their county because it will compete with their medical dispensary.

Second, there are the opportunistic individuals who view the license as a commodity. They never had the intention of starting their own business but had the foresight to anticipate the demand and hoped to cash in on the license rather than create a viable business.

While perhaps not a squatter in the more malicious or tactical sense described above, there are other people who really thought they could start a viable I-502 business, but only got far enough into the process to realize they lacked sufficient capital or the desire to transition into the new industry as they had originally anticipated.

They become squatters because they do not want to get out and forego the time, energy, effort, and money invested up to this point—they would like to get some compensation for it. Realizing now that there is a cap on the number of licenses available, they have a marketable, valuable product in the pending application, and want to sell it and potentially realize a gain.

PASS IT AROUND

A Secondary Market for Licenses

If you do not have a license but want to be in the marijuana industry, the only current option is to enter via the secondary market and join a pending or existing license. This is due to the LCB having closed the licensing window.

One thing that remains uncertain is whether the LCB will re-open the window due to the recent increase in the state canopy size from 2 million square feet to 8.5 million square feet. The LCB is going to have to create a way for the industry to scale up and there are a lot of different ways people speculate this might happen.

Originally when they conducted the lottery for applicants of producer/processor licenses, it was with the idea that each person, like the retailers, were going to have the option to have their name listed on three producer/processor licenses.

However, when the LCB saw the demand for licenses it was decided that they were going to reduce everybody to one license, with the additional two licenses being "on the shelf." Those with licenses "on the shelf" are supposedly grandfathered in, and will have the first opportunity in the event that additional licenses are granted to use one of those two licenses.

There is also currently a thirty percent cap on the individual license canopies. For instance, a Tier Three producer who is designated a thirty thousand square foot canopy is currently limited to a twenty one thousand square foot canopy. An alternative to granting more licenses would be removing the cap and allowing existing producers to operate at capacity.

However, it is unlikely this would meet the 8.5 million square foot canopy and additional licenses may ultimately be granted. Nonetheless, it is unknown what change will be made, if any, but the only current option for individuals to enter the industry is through the secondary market.

part six

WHERE ARE YOU GOING?

ZONING

Finding property, far and away, is the biggest challenge facing the industry. And perhaps magnifying this challenge more than anything is the zoning restrictions imposed at the county level. Zoning and land use is a complicated area, and it is important to start with an overview of how land may be designated as residential, industrial, agricultural, commercial, or otherwise.

One specific item making this so complex is the issue that simply because agriculture operations are allowed on a piece of property, this does not necessarily mean that marijuana is going to be allowed to operate on the same property. Marijuana is excluded from most agricultural definitions, so one cannot rely on this land use or zoning designation when locating a property. The best option in determining if a particular parcel is viable is to contact the LCB and county planning and development department. They have the final authority in determining whether land is suitable.

COUNTIES AND LAND USE

Each county will have its own code and marijuana operations may be permitted under many different land use designations—it may be residential, agricultural, industrial, commercial, etc. But whether or not a particular county is going to allow an operation will depend upon that particular county's system of rules.

The best example that we've seen is the Mason County Code, which goes through all the land use designations and provides for which designations are appropriate for an I-502 company. Further, it extends its requirements to indoor v. outdoor growing operations and whether a company is a producer, processor, or retailer. Mason County also provides subcategories within those mentioned above.

The land use designation we have found most problematic is generally what is classified as rural residential. This designation is in both Mason and Snohomish county—areas with sprawling rural land and few residential homes. Our understanding is this designation is used to preserve the rural nature of the land while maintaining some residential use. It is not for office parks, strip malls, or other commercial purposes. This becomes problematic with regard to marijuana as this would seem to preserve the rural feel of the land, but it interferes with the residential use.

Initially, some counties were open to producer/processors having this rural residential land use designation as a viable place for them to start their business. But what we have found in the past few months is counties are changing their codes and zoning-out companies with pending I-502 licenses.

UNANTICIPATED CHANGES IN LOCAL LAW

Mason County is an easy example of a county that passed laws, which could be interpreted as incentivizing marijuana operations, particularly producer/processors, to base their operations within the county. However, the county revised the regulations—after individuals and companies have purchased property and started improvements—and placed a moratorium on specific land use designations.

The purpose was to allow the county additional time to revisit the regulations and amend the county code and adjust the zoning restrictions. Specifically, the county revised the operations that were permitted on land designated as rural residential. This is just one of many similar code changes and moratoriums that have occurred within the state.

Snohomish County is another example we have encountered, which occurred after Mason County, but it was much more damaging. Mason County grandfathered in those companies that were already progressing through the application process; however, Snohomish County only permitted operations to continue if the final license had been obtained.

In both instances, your rights in terms of having a marijuana operation were vested. Snohomish County, though, specifically said if you try to expand your operations, you are going to lose those rights.

What is most shocking about these changes is how the rule changes have played out in each county. Given that Snohomish County zoned companies out of their property where they did not have a final license, a person or company could have spent $500,000 purchasing land and another $500,000 to retrofit the property for the I-502 operation. Until they get the final license from the state, meaning they have met all the state requirements, the counties can still come in, change zoning laws and prevent you from growing marijuana on the land you have spent one million dollars buying and improving.

ESTOPPEL "BUT THEY TOLD ME..."

Traditionally, there is a legal concept called estoppel, which would prevent the above scenario. It is the theory that a government person with authority to lead a person to believe that a certain activity would be permissible on a certain piece of property cannot thereafter prevent that person from conducting the activity where they have already changed their position in reliance on the advice and authority of the government person.

Currently, lawsuits on this very issue are working their way up the system—the city of Kent and the city of Fife. Most of the cities or counties trying to justify their bans or moratoriums are pointing toward federal law, saying that federal law preempts state law, but for the reason that we discussed earlier, a lot of those arguments are failing.

Another argument made by the cities is if states do not allow the bans, they are forcing the local jurisdictions to expend resources and enforce laws—identical to the state argument that the federal government cannot compel or commandeer the state to enforce the federal laws.

However, this argument fails at the local level because it is contrary to constitutional and state law. The federal government is a sovereign with limited powers, meaning that its powers are limited to powers that were specifically granted to it by the states at the time of formation. The thirteen colonies granted specific powers to the federal government, all other powers are reserved to the states.

Conversely, local jurisdictions, like counties and cities, are not sovereigns and they cannot say to the state government that they have retained authority or power to do certain things.

There are some state constitutions that allow local jurisdictions more autonomy, thereby giving them independence so long as they are not violating something at the state level. In other words, the statute acts as a floor or ceiling and local jurisdictions are permitted to draft their own interpretations that fall within the purview of the state statute.

One common question that arises when a state allows local governments to ban marijuana operations is whether voter intent is being thwarted. For instance, if every local jurisdiction elects to ban marijuana, despite the state statute for legalization, effectively it remains illegal. The obvious rebuttal argument is that this will not occur—every local municipality and county in the state is not going to ban marijuana; however, this still goes against the vote of the people. Inevitably, there would be a county opting to ban marijuana even where people voted for legalization.

This idea of thwarting the will of the people is a key argument. Opponents to this idea contend that I-502 has been poorly drafted in the sense that it did not account for the local opposition and there may be some weight to this argument as Oregon has attempted to avoid this very issue with its recently approved Measure 91.

THE GRASS IS GREENER: LOCAL LAW IN OTHER STATES

Measure 91 in Oregon specifically grants local jurisdictions the ability to vote on whether or not marijuana use is permitted. Unlike Washington, which is dealing with moratoriums and emergency ordinances, the system in Oregon requires a voter-approved prohibition, which specifically resolves the issue of thwarting the will of the people previously discussed.

COUNTIES

The Washington State Attorney General came out and made a comment, which although not binding, says that I-502, which legalized marijuana, provided no clear indication that it was intended to preempt local authority to regulate such businesses. They have concluded that I-502 still left the normal powers of local governments to regulate within their jurisdiction in place.

You can analogize or look to other situations, such as whether the state permits dry counties. Although federal law allows drinking, counties and states are free to prohibit alcohol as they see fit. The idea is that federal law has no bearing on a city or a county's authority to ban or permit a particular substance. States cannot draw or point to federal law. They have no authority to do that.

In guiding an investor who is considering putting money in this industry, it is important to consider whether the licensed operation is entering a city or county that may be considering a ban, moratorium, or whether current litigation is ongoing. Unfortunately, some of this may be unforeseeable. Using the counties political landscape and how I-502 was voted in, investors would have a strong place to start in determining whether a particular investment poses additional risks. It would be disingenuous to make any guarantees.

A FEW MORE DISCLAIMERS

It is probably a good time to note the importance of keeping up to date on current laws and regulations. By the time you are reading this book, much of the content may be already outdated.

At the state level, changes are more apparent, it is important to seek attorney advice when dealing with any local regulation. Zoning is perhaps the best example, as this requires more than looking at the county code and reviewing public records.

For example, we have spent weeks, if not months, researching parcels that seemed to be classified as rural residential on all zoning maps, but only a call to the Director of Planning and Development revealed the land was suitable for marijuana production due to a pre-existing use exception.

Moreover, this was a situation in which the county had recently amended its code so that marijuana production was not permitted on rural residential property. With so much information being available on the internet, it is easy to get lost in the weeds.

THE URBAN GROWTH ACT

Moving back into some of the zoning challenges, one immediate issue is with what is known as the Urban Growth Act (the "UGA"). The UGA provides additional layers of land use restrictions. Where the county may have three or four basic zones, the UGA may further classify those zones and place additional restrictions on what can be done in those areas.

The reason for the UGA is to focus on residential and commercial development. These get very tricky because they are a layer that is set on top of any existing land use regime. When researching the designation of a particular piece of land, you may easily find the urban growth area, which could have been put in place only five years ago, but fail to locate the original zoning designation.

The importance of understanding the different layers is so the UGA does not zone people out of their property. If land was used as a nursery prior to implementation of the UGA, the county may have provided for a legal nonconforming use. Which permits the original use to continue, even though it may not be permitted under the new UGA land use designation. Land use in almost every case is an authority designated from the state to the county and from the county to the cities.

In our experience, the method for zoning a UGA is not a scientific process. A county may have several zones that have been organized and a UGA that is overlaid on top of the existing zones. The UGA zones are generally determined according to the tax assessor records, treasurer records, or the existing use as determined by a county employee observing from the street.

If the person making the designation went out and saw nothing but residential houses and failed to see the nursery operating behind the property, the parcel may have been swept into a residential classification while it more accurately should have been designated as agricultural.

The most important thing to understand with zoning in general, and more specifically, the UGAs, is the importance of contacting the county officials themselves and requesting information. It is often thought to first contact the LCB, which is a good resource, but the county officials are also valuable in that they are intimately familiar with their own zoning requirements and county code, and can advise whether a particular parcel is suitable for I-502 use.

Keep in mind that as with most government officials, they are not permitted to give legal advice—so it is important to consult an attorney to determine whether a particular parcel in a particular county may be fruitful.

STATE AUTHORITY ON LOCAL GOVERNMENT

Despite the Attorney General's opinion that counties and cities are free to regulate I-502 companies under their own accord, the LCB has adopted the position that they will grant licenses without deference to county or city regulations. In other words, the state may not force the city to allow an operation, but the LCB is not going to withhold its grant of license simply because a city may be seeking to ban or prevent the operation.

Keep in mind this does not mean a person that obtains the LCB license or right to operate can then go in and operate in the city in violation of whatever the city rules are. They still have an obligation to independently seek and obtain whatever business licenses and permits are required at the county or city level.

Generally, the state and municipalities are deferring to each other—they are enforcing their own structure and regulations—making it important to perform your due diligence.

Cities

City limits must be considered when locating and determining what regulations must be followed. For example, the city of Arlington requires I-502 operations to obtain a city license and they have prohibited Tier Three producer operations. As such, any operation within the city limits must abide by these requirements.

However, a company operating beyond the city limits, despite having an Arlington address, will not be restricted to the same regulations. A mere couple of miles can dramatically shift what operations are permitted and what requirements must be met. Once again, this highlights the importance of checking all county and local laws before determining location.

FEDERAL LICENSING UNRELATED TO MARIJUANA

Keep in mind that there are multiple layers of legal requirements that have to be complied with—federal, state, county, and city—and it is important to understand that the recreational marijuana issue is going to impact and affect the operation at each of those levels. Earlier we provided a non-exhaustive list of federal agencies that are likely to take interest in an I-502 operation, and it is important to understand this relationship. Consider the USDA—marijuana may be banned at the federal level, but that does not mean a processing facility is exempt from complying with federal food handling requirements.

PROXIMITY THRESHOLDS

Property Setbacks

One of the most widely known requirements is the 1,000 foot setback from schools, playgrounds, recreation centers, childcare centers, public parks, public transit centers, libraries, or game arcades. This effort is in place to keep marijuana out of the hands of children. Most people are quickly made aware that there is a proximity setback requirement that is going to affect any operation, whether or not that operation is going to be approved by the LCB, or land use at the local level.

Minimum Distance Measurements

In practice, what does the minimum distance measurement actually mean? Does it mean the edge of the property needs to meet the 1,000 foot requirement? Is it the building itself that needs to meet the requirement?

Assume you have twenty acres and the building housing your entire operation is at the far end of property. It may be a long ways away in terms of the operation itself, but what if a park is adjacent to the other end of the property? Or what happens if a daycare goes in across the street after you have obtained your final license?

The current requirement is that the setback is based on the perimeter of the grounds and as the crow flies—meaning a straight line as opposed to common point of access. With regard to the daycare question, the restriction is limited to new marijuana licenses, so an existing marijuana operation will be vested in its rights.

Common Path of Egress

A common point of access is based on how a person could physically move from one access point to another. For example, if a marijuana operation is on a piece of property that abuts another piece of property on which a daycare is located, but there is no access without travelling a half mile, the common point of access would far exceed the 1,000 foot setback requirement. However, as the crow flies, the marijuana operation would be in violation because the properties would be adjacent to one another.

Gun Free Zones

It seems unlikely that the 1,000 foot setback itself will be changed, part of the reason this was established was due to the 1,000 foot drug free school zone. It is a heightened criminal penalty for selling drugs on the street corner within 1,000 feet of a schoolyard. However, this also raises the question of whether the 1,000 foot setback undermines the purpose of the I-502 implemented setback.

The original setback was designed to discourage and displace illegal activities, but here, the setback is displacing legal activities. Nonetheless, it upholds the purpose of keeping drugs, legal and illegal, out of the hands of children.

Drug free zones and setbacks also raise the interesting issue of how the state will deal with any amended regulation. For instance, up to this point the existing operations have had to tailor everything around a strict implementation; however, any dramatic changes would give new entrants to the market an advantage, such as better locations.

Pre-Designated Zones

One of the ideas that has been floating in some of the municipalities is whether to have designated areas for I-502 operations. If the city has predetermined or pre-zoned an area for I-502 companies, it would greatly simplify the cost of approval for the city, who currently has to review a piece of property from every angle, by making that predetermination. Alternatively, this would create districts, which may become less desirable.

Timing Measurements

At this point, the position that has been adopted is that the state cannot displace an operation which has received its final issue or permit. If you were, for example, to have provided information or evidence to the LCB, which was accurate at that time, that there was no daycare in proximity, the LCB would not retroactively deny a license.

It starts to make more sense when you think about why there is distinction between a licensed daycare and an unlicensed daycare, and part of that is notice. Is there a recreational marijuana retail shop on notice that there's a daycare in the area, and if it isn't a licensed daycare, it's a lot more difficult for them to have been put on notice to know that there may have been a daycare. And vice versa.

Right now there are no waivers or variances of any kind that allow an I-502 operation to break the 1,000 foot setback requirement. Eventually, there probably will be a variance process where there are situations where it is not necessarily applicable. Say, for example, there is a body of water that is not crossable— you are 900 feet away from something else, but there's a body of water which absolutely would prohibit anybody from crossing over it.

Is the 1,000 foot proximity really appropriate in that instance? It is supposed to be a matter of accessibility to anybody who may be in that location. However, at this point in time, there is no variance provisions, at either the state or local level for this requirement, so a waiver is not an option.

NEW TO THE NEIGHBORHOOD

Minimize the Risk of Opposition

In finding a suitable location, if there's a notice of any kind of potential issue that may occur, whether now or at a later point in time, my advice is going to be to look somewhere else. There are a lot of places out there in the state that are available. The obstacle that people are encountering is that they go into a place thinking that it was OK, and then an issue arises later. What you want to do is minimize future obstacles by looking for and investigating the common issues that people have encountered.

What is the amount of risk I may face by going after a particular property? Factors like that, obviously, should be deterring a person from wanting to go in. Alternatively, if you already own your property and are considering the existing risks, the financial risk may be a lot lower and it might warrant pursuing. There are going to be fact-specific variables in any given situation which are going to help a person make that determination.

DUE DILIGENCE ON PROPERTY

All of this emphasizes the importance of due diligence. If you're looking at a piece of property and you're entering into a Letter of Intent, give yourself time to check every possible detail and confirm the location with both the county planning and development department and the LCB.

LETTERS OF INTENT

A Letter of Intent (LOI) is a common document, which is entered into by parties who want to sell or buy a piece of property, or similar type business arrangement. However, unlike a final agreement, the LOI provides general terms and is mostly non-binding. It provides a starting point or foundation for future negotiations.

The LOI is a great example of something that does not take long for an attorney to prepare, thus does not cost much money, but it will provide solutions to dozens of issues that may not have been apparent to either party initially. It will save you a lot of money in the long run as it allows you to avoid potential pitfalls and disputes because you are aware of what needs to be investigated during a due diligence period.

This is especially important for an operation that plans to lease its property instead of purchase for its own usage. When purchasing property there is a formal purchase and sale agreement, which provides a period of time where the buying party can investigate the property. This is known as "due diligence." Leasing property is often less formal but a similar due diligence should be conducted. While you are no longer determining whether you want to purchase the property, you must still determine whether the property is suitable for your operation.

We have already dealt with one instance where the parties did not use the LOI and immediately executed a binding lease agreement. It was later found that the land was not suitable for the I-502 operation and currently the parties are disputing some of the terms in the lease.

It is also important to understand that you cannot keep your business a secret. One of the first steps in the process is providing notice to the city. You may buy the property and attempt to keep the operation under the radar, but as soon as the process begins with the LCB, the community receives notification that a marijuana business will be located in the community. This emphasizes the importance of transparency—which might include reaching out to neighbors to measure their position on recreational marijuana laws before a problem arises.

It is far better to find this information early in the process and not learn of angry neighbors after investing in the property. This is not to suggest that neighbors can prohibit your operation if you meet all the state and local requirements, but these are commonly the situations that ultimately start discussions about local and county moratoriums and zoning changes.

ADVANTAGES OF TRANSPARENCY

We are a business-planning firm, which means that our goal is to help individuals properly plan their business venture and avoid litigation or disputes in the future. It saves money, stress, time, and energy for everybody involved.

We approach it from a strategic perspective, minimizing risk and maximizing potential for a return on the investment. With the LCB, one of the strategies that we have found to be very effective, but not necessarily a prevalent attitude among many people up to this point, is transparency and disclosure with all interested parties.

Neighbors

It may seem counter-intuitive to knock on the doors of all of the neighbors surrounding a piece of property before you purchase it in order to tell them what it is that you want to do with it, but it is not a bad idea in this industry.

This may simply mean sending a letter introducing yourself, explaining what you are doing and how you plan to be a good steward. Not only does this provide notice, but it also opens the line of communication. It is also a much easier way to learn if you have a potentially problematic neighbor who plans to spend his life savings fighting against you.

PRINCIPLE V. PROFIT

Security

There are specific requirements that the LCB requires and this is where a lot of the initial capital will be focused for new I-502 businesses. After qualification of the parties of interest and financiers related to a license, one of the next biggest considerations is going to be property compliance. This includes a wide range of things, such as setbacks from properties, fencing, security cameras, and recording.

Fences

All I-502 producer operations must be obscured from public view and for outdoor growing operations this requires a fence that is at least eight feet high. Alternatively, indoor operations do not require a fence so long as it takes place within a fully enclosed secure indoor facility or greenhouse with rigid walls, a roof, and doors.

Street Visibility

Fences and public visibility is an example where there are a lot of different strategic approaches when considering location and type of indoor v. outdoor grow operation. There are people who, in racing towards revenue, have put up temporary fences to save time and money. However, when the fence starts to decay or is damaged in a storm, they are no longer in compliance and could have their license suspended or, in more reckless situations, revoked altogether. Whereas, someone who opts for a decent quality fence is less likely to encounter an issue.

BUFFER AREAS AND BEAUTY FENCES

Further steps that some people have used when building their operation is a security buffer or a clear area between the fences. Some municipalities will have limits on the height of the fence that can be erected within sight of the neighbors. Eight feet sometimes will exceed that height—it may be a six-foot limitation.

The municipality wants to avoid the appearance of having a compound. What some of our clients have done is erect an eight-foot fence as near proximity to the operation as is practical. They set-out a ten, fifteen, or twenty foot clear area and erected a more aesthetically pleasing six or five-foot fence.

Not only does this meet city requirements, but line of sight also allows for a more aesthetically appealing look—one that does not appear as a marijuana factory or compound. Additionally, you are going to have fewer issues from neighbors when they see that you're putting a beautiful fence up and improving the aesthetics of the property.

CRIME VICTIM RECOURSE— ACCESS TO LAW ENFORCEMENT

Remember, the person who is more likely to become the victim of crime is less likely to be somebody who is operating legally within the bounds of the law and who may have some form of recourse if somebody commits a crime as opposed to somebody who may be operating illegally.

I use the analogy that heavy concentrations of undocumented worker populations generally have much higher crime rates, not because there's a greater criminal disposition, but because they may have fewer avenues of recourse. They are less inclined to call the police in order to come and have the criminal arrested. By legalizing marijuana, you can start to see how it makes sense that marijuana related crime would probably decrease. There is more likely to be a penalty for a criminal perpetuating a crime in that area because the victim can call the police for assistance.

It is also important to understand the projection your business may have. When you are doing this outreach with communities, you want to let them know that you are developing the property in such a way that it does not advertise itself as a marijuana production facility. You have security and you are building it in such a way that nobody really has to know what's going on in there. This relates to the idea of strategic planning.

SECURITY VIDEO SURVEILLANCE

In considering the security surveillance requirements, all operations must have cameras and there cannot be any place in the facility larger than one square foot that is not monitored by a video camera.

Additionally, the camera must have a minimum pixel resolution of 640 × 470, record no less than thirty frames per second, and twenty-four hours a day, with forty-five days of video backup maintained. The security video surveillance requirement only applies to entrances and exits, grow canopy areas, the processing areas, storage areas, and any other area where the marijuana may be produced, processed, transported, and stored.

NUISANCE

Noxious Odor

Odor is one of the complaints that have been raised by opponents to the industry. Whether or not odor is actually an issue is going to depend on the strain of marijuana and the type of structure being used. For example, an outdoor grow operation that has constant ventilation, may not have much odor.

Whereas an enclosed grow operation, using carbon dioxide and is sealed twenty hours of the day with a high concentration ventilation during a very narrow period of time, might have a stronger odor. Filters are a solution which may prevent odors for indoor grow operations altogether. The bottom line is that this is a very fact-specific analysis and will vary from operation to operation. The other thing about smell is that it is extremely subjective.

Light Pollution

Another potential nuisance issue is light pollution. For example, there may be light on the premises at off-peak hours. A lot of our clients grow on a twelve-hour cycle this is commonly between the hours of 10:00 PM and 10:00 AM when normally you would not expect to see a lot of light. The reason for the off-peak hours is to utilize cheaper electricity rates, but it is also easier to control your own light and not rely on natural light.

Environmental Contaminants/Toxicity: Fertilizers and Pesticides

Generally, there are fewer uses of synthetic pesticides and lower concentrations of synthetic fertilizers due to the method of consumption. What you would consider organic growth methods are used much more often in the production or processing of marijuana. You are providing a product that is smoked as-is. You cannot spray it down with a chemical and then expect people to burn it and inhale it.

Also, most of the processes which are widely used at this point, particularly for indoor grow operations, use a reclamation process. They are catching and trying to reuse as much of the residual chemicals, fertilizer, soil, and water in the course of their production process than a lot of other more traditional agricultural methods.

WATER CONSUMPTION

The thing to remember is that growing marijuana is no different from any other agricultural operation—water consumption is going to be impactful. The best thing a company can do is be transparent and mitigate water usage as much as possible. If you do have a bad neighbor who may be irrational, you just have to make sure you are staying within the law.

That is why, in a business planning approach, one of the things we advise clients to do is to take a head-down approach. Meaning you are not always going to be able to plan for every contingency.

Mason County provides another good example of keeping a head-down approach. There was a particular producer/processor who was already operating, and while their operation was not crossing the line, the quality of their fencing skirted up against what was permitted. The county used them as an example and their name was used in the public records and hearings. No company wants this type of recognition or notoriety, so staying as far from any lines as possible is always the recommended course of action.

part seven

LOCATION
LOCATION
LOCATION

ENVIRONMENTAL

Potential Environmental Impact Issues

There are no specific I-502 regulations, but there are city and county regulations that must be taken into consideration when locating property.

It is simply another example of why finding location is the single most difficult component for a new I-502 operation. A prime example is what we have experienced in Snohomish County. They have a lot of ponds and lakes that are designated as wetlands.

Wetlands and Sensitive Areas

The natural abundance of rivers, lakes, and streams here in the Pacific Northwest is an integral part of our beautiful landscape. Beneath the surface of all that beauty, however, could lurk a mess of restrictions on a property's new use development or an attempt to expand its existing use.

Even where there are signs that water is merely seasonal or occurs with the occasional flood, simply dumping in fill dirt and building on top may not be an option. At the very least, if such development is permitted, land-owners should be prepared for mitigation requirements as a condition of building approval. When in doubt, a preliminary Environmental Impact Study (EIS) might be prudent before getting locked into the property—an EIS is performed by licensed engineers and can sometimes come at a price that exceeds the combined total of all other costs associated with the property purchase transaction.

Mitigation Measures

Like the EIS, the cost of actual mitigation, which may be a condition to permitted use, can more easily double the final cost of a given project. All prudent businesses should plan to investigate potential wetland and sensitive area issues as a basic part of their due diligence well before jumping into any property purchase.

As a point of reference, one recent client who owns a five-acre parcel in a rural Eastern Washington county, zoned agricultural, will incur expenses of around $20,000 in direct costs to obtain the EIS.

Seasonal Timing

The season or time of year can actually affect when an environmental impact study may be conducted. If you end up purchasing a piece of property in August or September, it may be March or April before you can even have a satisfactory environmental impact study conducted by a qualified engineering firm. Another point to consider—these are not things you want to find out after you have purchased the property.

Adding insult to injury in the previous example, the client in that case was also required to wait nine months before the necessary seasonal conditions would be present for engineers to begin the study. The indirect cost of the delay in this case far exceeded the direct cost of the EIS. Remember, however, this is only a single example. The ultimate feasibility of a project will depend on the cost and timing, but also subject to the applicable laws. These determinations must be made based on the unique conditions, which vary widely, for every piece of property.

Conditions of Usage

If there is concern regarding a particular wetland or the need for an environmental impact study, it is important to check records during the due diligence period. Oftentimes, environmental impact studies have been conducted at some point in time and a study conducted ten years ago still could be relevant and may answer a lot of your questions.

It is another term for your Letter Of Intent— what documents you request from the potential seller. Environmental documents should be available from the seller, and in the event they are not, they should have information about who conducted the EIS and where the information is available.

The interesting point here is that in other industries, it is common for a person to be obtaining a mortgage on a piece of property. However, by necessity in the I-502 industry, people typically obtain some form of nonconventional financing, such as the owner carrying a promissory note. As a result, some of the safeguards put in place by mortgage companies might get be overlooked.

People were not finding out until after paying cash for their property, and thinking they got a great deal, that issues may have been brought to their attention if they had started the business through more conventional means. Conforming to building codes and retrofitting is a huge expense that must be considered. This again highlights the importance of talking with an attorney and doing your due diligence.

GROW LIGHTS

Grow lights are just one example of retrofitting that is required, but electricity in general is one of the most expensive upgrades. Transformers, which were discussed earlier, may cost upwards of $100,000. And lights cannot simply be purchased from your local hardware store. Proper grow lights are required and they may cost over $100 per unit.

EXTRACTORS AND SPECIALIZED EQUIPMENT

Extractors are another huge, albeit optional, expense. Most of our clients are selecting the same brand, and often exceed $100,000. The point is that the materials required to retrofit a building are not items you can find locally, and you cannot get proper equipment at budget friendly prices.

Growing marijuana is expensive and this must be considered when selecting property and choosing the type of operation you want to have. However, this also highlights why investment opportunities are available.

Along with electricity, lights and extractors, another retrofitting expense that people face is the light-blocking infrastructure in greenhouses. Again considering the grow cycle is typically twelve hours and greenhouses allow for natural light, there must be a structure in place to block out all lights.

While not every operation will run the same cycle, some consider controlling light availability to the plants down to the minute.

Additionally, building a blackout transition room is another consideration—this is where you enter a vestibule area with a double-doored structure that closes, blacks out, and then you pass through a second set of doors when you go into it. There are also green lights, which allow you to see in the growing room, but do not induce flowering.

part eight

RED TO BLACK TO GREEN

ARE YOU IN OR OUT?

Chart a Route to Profitability Early in the Process

Indoor v. outdoor growth and definitions of each is an important consideration. Outdoor grows are further divided into two categories, which are subject to different licensing processes and sometimes local zoning regulations: (1) greenhouses and (2) open-air.

If you are purchasing a piece of property and are intending to build greenhouses, you may have to obtain local permits because they are considered a permanent improvement to the property. A definition of what is a temporary or permanent structure is going to vary and this is often the threshold of when permits are required. This varies dramatically from one county to another. Examples of the threshold may be pouring foundation versus merely pouring a concrete slab. This is an important delineation if you are planning any additional greenhouses as it may reveal hidden costs.

You need to plan for what it may cost to install a greenhouse on the property. It is going to be based on more factors than simply how much the greenhouse itself is going to cost to install. Not only the labor and materials but also how much is it going to cost to erect that structure. We mentioned already environmental impact studies.

It is an example of where you are improving the property, a temporary versus a permanent structure may be a determining factor as to whether or not you need to obtain an environmental impact study before erecting a structure itself. A structure that may cost you $100,000 to erect could ultimately cost an additional $20,000 to $40,000 when you factor in an environmental impact study, local permit, and inspection.

Common permitting inspection processes might include fence permits, septic tanks, and wells. You may have water quality inspections as well. This is aside and separate from USDA requirements depending on where you are located. In some locations, the state already performs water quality testing annually. It depends on what the requirements are in the county where you are operating.

For a transformer, you will need a licensed electrician to come out and perform the inspection. Normally, equipment like a transformer that is sold through an approved vendor by the utility company may have limited options in terms of who you can purchase equipment from and who may install the equipment at your location.

It is a legalized monopoly and there may only be one supplier. Some of this equipment is so specialized that it is not a matter of simply having somebody show up to hook it up next week or next month, there may be back orders for installation that could delay an operation for months.

It is important to consider what permits may be required and the type of operation you want to have. In some instances it may be beneficial to utilize structures that avoid timely and costly permits.

However, there are also many other reasons why obtaining the necessary permits and building permanent structures is recommended. Ultimately, it is a very fact intensive determination, but one that must be decided before the operation commences.

LABOR—EMPLOYEES

Let me just mention scalability, because I think it is a significant point for anybody who is thinking about getting into this industry. There are a lot of people out there who have the knowledge and expertise on managing and growing marijuana—usually at a very small scale.

But the scalability, the size of these I-502 operations at 20,000 or more square feet, that is new. There are far fewer resources out there for figuring out how exactly to do this. This is an area that anybody hoping to get into the industry needs to realize has a lot of pitfalls.

There is a huge learning curve and the more access they have to reliable information on avoiding some of the expensive learning processes, the better off they're going to be. There have been a lot of expensive lessons for a lot of people who are trying to get their operation set up.

This goes back to location of property. Clients have had so many obstacles and things pop up, and one of them is water quality. The most recent incident we have encountered involved the USDA. A food-processing license was denied based on water quality—the chloroform count in the well was fractionally too high. As a result, a two-week purification process was required.

Labor & Employment

You will have to think about whether your operation requires you to choose to either hire regular or contract employees, and where the employees are located—professional employment agencies, referrals, or possibly through online advertising.

Some of the traditional options, particularly for startups using contract labor, are limited and controlled. You need to give some forethought and consideration if you are thinking about using a contractor or outside labor.

Anybody from Office Depot, down to your employment company might use either temporary labor, agencies, or employment companies who will manage everything from the screening, interviewing, hiring, human resources, withholdings, and printing the paychecks. These employment agencies simplify the process with a person who merely shows up and provides the labor.

There are very important limitations on what an I-502 operation is going to be allowed to do regarding contract labor. There is not the same degree of flexibility that may be available to other businesses where there is less of a learning curve.

You pay a premium price for getting those employment services, but for most small companies in a new industry, they need a lot of labor brought in very quickly. It is generally worth the premium cost because you might have the business expertise, but lack the human resources expertise and knowledge of the related labor laws. There are also companies that are specializing in providing turnkey and consulting services—providing all the services necessary for an operation to come in and begin growing and processing marijuana.

The idea of providing a turnkey operation or consulting service is similar to how we help our clients. They are very familiar with the process. They streamline everything that is required to get up to final licensing. They have contracts with some employees so they can assist with some of the purchase deals. The issues the turnkey operations face are that they are trying to do compensation based off of profits.

They are really skirting up against the edges because they are at the threshold of acting like owners. Another huge disadvantage is that because the employment agencies are not attorneys, there are huge limitations on what they can advise. Such as, the business documents they can prepare—they cannot draft all the documents.

That is one of the most important aspects. Dealing with the LCB as legal counsel, the drafting of documents, reviewing of documents, assisting with the negotiation of all these various things is a smoother process. The consulting company might be able to sit down and suggest what products will be useful and what space is needed, but they cannot provide legal advice when navigating I-502 in the state of Washington.

FINAL EMPLOYMENT CONSIDERATIONS

Another additional consideration is the importance of the employee handbook. Specifically, employers should carefully craft intoxication provisions. As stated from the outset of this book, if you are looking for an easy way to obtain marijuana, just like owning or operating an I-502 company is not a good way to get cheap marijuana, the same applies to employees. Keep in mind all the traceability and security requirements discussed. Employees will need to obtain marijuana from retail stores, just like any ordinary consumer.

This also extends beyond the intoxication into the degree and scope of authority that an employee may have to take action on behalf of the company. Something to keep in mind, we have at least one instance where an employee placed an order for supplies for the company, which may not seem that unusual. A lot of employees have the authority, ability, and access to funds for the company to place an order for supplies that the company needs, such as paper, pens and pencils, or a toner cartridge.

In this instance, however, due to it being an I-502 company, they were trying to place an order for plants, which was outside of the scope and authority of crossing state lines. The employee far overstepped what was legal and permitted for that employee to do.

Fortunately, the employer/client in this case caught it before the order was official, the goods were shipped, or any money had changed hands. The reason it was even brought to their attention was due to the credit card company flagging it and contacting them to inquire about the transaction.

Employee agreements are also an issue with hourly employees at the $15 to $20 an hour rate. Normally, an employer might not spend the time, money, or invest in an employee agreement. However, it may be something worth considering in this instance because you may have someone who may be trimming or handling the product and the company has very specific responsibilities in terms of tracking that product from seed to sale.

It may be worth the extra money it would take to invest in even a standardized employee agreement in addition to any standard confidentiality, trade secret, non-disclosure, and non-competition agreements an employer might want to adopt. This is something that, depending on how much detail is being put into this, is probably worth putting at least a little bit of time into researching what is required.

As discussed, with trade secrets there isn't a required registration like with a trademark or patent. Trade secrets are all about how you actually protect it and keep the recipe or operation a secret. If you terminate someone's employment, you do not want him or her to disseminate the company's trade secrets to a new employer.

If they are a well-established employee with a very specific set of skills, there is a good chance whey will end up performing a similar role for a competitor or smaller company. This is where trade secret protection and noncompete agreements are important. Often-times, by taking the initial step of having the agreements is all the prevention necessary to establish that dissemination is prohibited. In my experience, the majority of these particular problems arise more as product of an accident, rather than as the product of some malicious intent or disloyalty.

Generally, everyone entering into any relationship has the best of intentions and optimism, whether it is the employer, employee, or business associates, but protecting against all avoidable issues is important.

INDUSTRY INSIGHT:
TOP TEN ISSUES WITH SCALE

Jason Smit, MASTER GROWER

Avitas Agriculture, Inc., Tier 2 Producer / Processor

This list is coming from the perspective of a successful medical marijuana grower transitioning to the new recreational laws. It is not in order. Like a successful growing formula, every part contributes to the overall success of the formula. None of these things are to be considered as the final truth, but none of them are trivial.

1. Know your Strengths and Weaknesses

Are you a business person? Are you a grower? Surround yourself with people who will complement your strengths and weaknesses. Surround yourself with people who will challenge your assumptions. Be prepared to defend your assumptions, but don't be unwilling to compromise.

2. Don't Change Successful Growing Formulas

For example, if you've never grown in a greenhouse, don't start out in a greenhouse for your legal business. Instead, take your winning formula and multiply that to start your legal business. Once you have duplicated this success at a larger scale, gradually change things to improve costs and efficiency. Growing is not magic; it is about the scientific method. You must isolate variables and keep them constant to sustain success.

3. Don't Bite off More Than you can Chew

As a general rule of thumb, multiply your winning formula by five to start out. This is important to cut your losses if you aren't successful. You will need to deal with much more than just growing as you scale. Resist the temptation to go much farther than where you have been right away. This includes the space where you start.

4. Design and Build

Contact your local building department immediately and do not hide any aspect of your plan. I cannot stress this enough. Six months after we contacted the county to start our building permit application, they changed the rules and did not allow any other growers to start the process. Almost 90 potential growers are currently impacted. Strongly consider hiring a use expert to help you with this process. Involve all parties during the design of the grow space. The grower needs this space to be his. Building and materials are costly and it will be four times as costly if you need to redo things. Get a lot of bids for every phase of the project you will not do yourself.

5. Schedule and Budget

Any residential builder will tell you a standard project will take twice as long as you initially estimate. I have heard commercial builders tell me things take four times as long. It took us 11 months to get our commercial building permits from the county, but we were converting a single family residence to a commercial space. I would imagine an existing commercial space would take half that time. Plan accordingly with your schedule. Similarly, your budget will be impacted as well. There are a hundred things that will come up that you simply won't think of if you are doing anything for the first time. Also, beware of gouging by unscrupulous contractors. Our electrical bids varied from $100K to $40K. Our fire prevention plan varied from $150K to $4K.

6. Locating the Space

Contact your local planning department immediately and tell them your plans. Work with them during your property search; I cannot stress this enough. There are many things to consider when finding your space. Friendly landlords, unfriendly neighbors, availability of utilities, cost of utilities, quality of water, city or county jurisdiction, setback and zoning rules, expansion capability, political climate, fire prevention access, need for odor control, etc. Obviously agriculture zones are a natural location but how is the political climate? Are the water rights encumbered by federal regulations? How is the situation politically? Finally, be prepared for changes.

7. Distribution

How will you get rid of 50 lbs. a week if you are used to growing 2 lbs. a week? One cannot underestimate how cutthroat marijuana distribution is. There are a hundred other growers trying to sell their product and if they have been willing to break the law in the past, they will do whatever it takes to sell their product legally as well. One should strongly consider having a dedicated salesman who knows the ins and outs of cannabis industry distribution.

8. Rules and Regulations

People who are used to underground cultivation, or a loose medical marijuana industry, might not be aware of all the rules and regulations involved in the legal system. Don't approach the regulatory hurdles with a distrust of authority. Any working relationship must go both ways. Currently, the federal government is letting the legal states operate, but if they don't like how the whole experiment is going, they could change their minds. For this reason we must set aside our preconceptions and work together. Resist the temptation to bend any rule, no matter how small or insignificant they may seem to be. The future of legal marijuana depends on us.

9. Hiring People

You will need help running your business. Friends and family will want to be a part of this, but be careful with friends and family. Do they have experience with the jobs they are expected to perform? Do they have professional work experience? Friends and family will be much harder to part ways with if things are not working out. You will also want to bring in other people; either professional contacts or hiring from the outside. Consider adopting a standardized interview process.

10. Networking

Meeting new people should be a part of any plan to be successful. Some of your friends from the medical industry may not make it. Step outside of your comfort zone and network.

INSURANCE

Insurance is really simple and we have not yet had any clients run up against this issue. Our clients have not been using traditional financing sources, like a mortgage. A mortgage company would require a mortgagee to carry property insurance that would cover destruction of the structure or replacement value.

A lot of operations are not required by a third party to carry that type of insurance. It may not occur to them, or they may choose not to try and obtain it, but if you have cash tied up in an asset like that, it really behooves you to investigate whether it may be worth the relatively small cost.

The state is already going to require you to cover all insurance for labor and industry purposes. For example, you may need to invest in slip and fall insurance for people who may be visiting the property. It would be terrible to have a company pulling in millions of dollars only to turn around and lose that money because of a simple injury. As we talk about slip and fall insurance, there is another document that we have dealt with and that is a waiver and release. This waiver releases liability for employees and for anyone visiting the property.

Some of this starts moving into structuring, protection of assets, and use of business entities in order to distribute cash assets or properties. It may not be in a company's interest to pay cash and then hold their own real property. Particularly, where there is a specific exemption built into the law for separating out the use of property and payment to the property holder.

The insurance industry is a heavily regulated industry. Most insurance companies cross state borders so they are dealing with federal and state regulations. Some insurance companies are shying away from wanting to insure any of the operations relating to I-502.

They have the risk of exposure to federal seizure. The insurance company may want to structure special provisions into the agreement depending on the nature of the business operation. Any company that is providing general business liability insurance, property liability, or personal injury insurance goes under the nature of the business.

If you are an investor or a financier who is lending money to an I-502 operation intending to take a security interest in the property itself, your expectation is for them to be carrying property liability insurance to insure against loss of that property. You better be sure that they can actually obtain that insurance for their operation. Also, confirm that they are actually carrying that insurance.

DISTRIBUTION CHANNELS

There are special rules and requirements governing the method of distribution and transportation of product between entities. For both internal company operations and also for transportation of goods with other business, there are specific requirements regarding the use of trucks.

You cannot use an open van, which you may traditionally think would be a great way to transport product. It has to be a truck with a separate cab. The actual storage container itself must be physically attached to the vehicle frame, so you cannot simply put everything into a box that sits in the back of the truck. It needs to be in a container that is secured to the truck itself. There cannot be windows in the cargo compartment area and there also cannot be branding on the truck.

When making distributions between the producer and processor, or processor and the retail location, you cannot make intermediary stops. Your driver cannot stop for lunch while delivering the product. He cannot even stop at the attorney's office mid route to sign some documents. They are allowed only specific intermittent stops. It is important that people familiarize themselves with the exact requirements. For a lot of these policies to be upheld, everyone involved needs to be intimately educated and this is where the employee handbook comes into play.

If you know who your delivery driver will be, ensure the person has read and understands the terms in your handbook. It is not going to do you any good as the owner of the company to familiarize yourself with what the requirements are if in turn you do not educate your driver on those same requirements. You cannot expect the driver to comply with the laws if you have not actually confirmed that they have been educated on what the laws are.

Make sure everyone signs a page at the end of the handbook that ensures that they have read every last word, because that is what you are going to be leaning on if one of your truck drivers gets caught violating the regulations.

MERCHANDISING & MARKETING

This is a huge area where people can get into trouble—the idea that no licensee (a producer, processor or a retailer) can sell merchandise with their branded name or logo on it. For example, a producer cannot go out and sell or give away promotional items with their logo on it, it is not allowed by licensees.

However, the Liquor Control Board (LCB) has specifically stated that you can enter into a license agreement with a separate company who then could sell branded merchandise. One caveat to all this is that paraphernalia, which is vapor pens, glass, pipes, bongs, and hookahs, is one area that you cannot put your brand or logo on the product.

One thing that I should clarify is that paraphernalia with your brand logo can be sold to retailers to sell. However, promotional items cannot be given away with your brand logo, regardless of branded merchandise, paraphernalia or otherwise. If you happen to unfortunately, inadvertently, accidentally, or ignorantly violate a rule or procedure, there are steps a company ought to take in order to minimize the potential risk of repercussions, fines or penalties and going as far as outright termination of the permit.

Depending on the nature of the violation and the extent of the violation that may have occurred, the recourse or action a company may want to take in order to minimize its exposure may be outright disclosure to the LCB, with the steps that have been taken to minimize risk that this might occur again in the future.

Reemphasizing the importance of being upfront throughout the entire process, it really does mitigate the issue. The LCB has so much latitude or discretion in regards to resolving or dealing with issues at this point, based largely upon the fact that there is no precedent they are going to be looking into each circumstance specifically. Was the violation inadvertent? Was it something that even if they did not know was a violation, should they have known? What mitigation steps were taken after the fact? How prompt were they in making a correction? How forthcoming were they in correcting it? These are all questions the LCB will ask.

In most instances, the LCB has a huge interest in ensuring the success of companies that have demonstrated a desire to operate within the system that has been established. For a company that may have violated a rule, the LCB has an interest in companies trying to make corrections so that they can operate within the system—to help those companies succeed and provide a means for those companies to succeed. Far more so than a company that may be breaking those rules and trying to find ways to operate outside of rules and try to avoid getting caught. Those people are much more likely to get pushed out of the industry.

My experience today, as I have mentioned several times, is that the LCB, for the most part, is interested in ensuring the compliance of companies, not simply catching the non-compliance of companies in order to penalize them. This should be distinguished, too, from the LCB being proactive in order to promote the development of the industry.

What they are interested in doing is promoting a successful, but legal industry, over the illicit industry and in promoting people who have demonstrated that they are going to bring that sense of legitimacy and compliance to the company.

part nine

STRATEGIC PLANNING

THE BUSINESS END OF THINGS

Our firm's marijuana business planning strategy is to make sure you are not the company that is made an example of how not to act, regardless of whether or not you are actually in violation of a rule. I think strategically, it usually works to your advantage to try and stay as far away from the legal line as you can. It may not be any more expensive than coming up against the line of legal versus illegal, when you factor in the increased degree of risk that you may spend if you end up relocating after you get zoned out of your property or if you end up in a legal battle.

Incidentally, in Snohomish County, if you look at the public hearings, there seems to be a single individual—a very wealthy individual—with a lot of financial and political resources. He has been driving much of the public discourse, opposition, and changes, which most recently have resulted in local moratoriums banning operations on certain land use designation. Do not discount the power and influence that a single individual or business may have on your operation.

The best way to find out whether or not you might be at risk is by simply talking to the neighbors—disclose what you are doing. Go out of your way to let them know a little about what you're doing. They are going to find out anyway.

It's better to avoid buying the land and investing a million dollars, only to find out later that there's a difficult neighbor next door with the means to make the process more difficult. If you're already moved in, consider having an attorney familiar with I-502 draft a letter of introduction. It'll be to your advantage in the long run.

Even filing an answer to a complaint may be more costly than contacting an attorney for a proper LOI. For instance, a neighbor may file a complaint against you for something utterly absurd and ridiculous. Merely filing an answer to that complaint, and getting the complaint dismissed, will likely cost you more money than the LOI would have cost you in the first place. Consider it insurance. It's an inexpensive insurance policy to put a $5,000 or $10,000 advance deposit with an attorney compared to possibly double that cost in dealing with a lawsuit or aggressive neighbor.

INDUSTRY INSIGHT:
TOP TEN I-502 SURPRISES
Alex and Becky Hutton
Seattle Sound LLC, Tier 2 Producer/Processor

1. Scale

There is no starting small and scaling up by reinvesting profits. LCB wants a full build out for licensing.

2. Leases

Renting a site location is a challenging option. There is a lot of price gouging in I-502 compliant/desired commercial spaces, so owning a building outright is ideal.

3. Capital

Startup costs are significantly higher than expected. Space needs to be secured months before the application is even processed.

4. Harvest Planning

As a single business entity, traditional tri-monthly harvesting does not work. Retail stores need product to be on a more frequent schedule.

5. Business

Traditional business rules and suppositions do not apply to I-502. A majority of people in this industry come from non-business backgrounds.

6. Government

There are multiple governing bodies besides the LCB that will require a variety of licenses and permits before operations commence. Federal, state, city, county, and the health department all have a say in your I-502 business.

7. Quicksand

It seems the laws and rules are constantly changing. Sometimes it feels impossible to keep them straight despite the number of hours spent researching.

8. Banking

Not every professional welcomes I-502 money. Many banks, accountants, landlords, cities, insurance companies, and real estate agencies have refused to work with I-502 businesses.

9. Viewpoints

Sometimes it feels like disagreement among I-502 business people devolves into petty bickering—occasionally even ending in people refusing to do business with each other because of diverging views on the pursuit of profit.

10. Cohesion

Although there are plenty of I-502 groups and associations, most remain small and ineffective with little to no influence at the state level.

ENTITY FORMATION: LLC V. CORPORATION

One of the areas specific to the I-502 industry that we have had to spend a lot of time planning is related to estate planning and intestate situations. More specifically, a situation where an individual dies without a will, and the ownership of the company interest could pass to an individual who may not be qualified with the LCB.

This person ends up an owner of the LLC membership interest. They do not qualify, and the permit, which has been issued, is suspended, terminated, or the status is in violation of LCB rules because this person was not qualified prior to the transfer of ownership. Planning for, and anticipating those types of scenarios is really important.

Another situation to plan for is divorce. Washington is a community property state, which means that any assets acquired after the formation of the marriage are commonly owned between the spouses. This why the LCB is requiring that spouses meet all of its qualifications. Where a divorce occurs, a spouse whose intention was not to be a direct owner or to have any say in the operations of the company ends up with a significant portion of ownership of the company. And so, the LCB wants to ensure that the license is not jeopardized.

Two different points immediately come to mind with regard to spousal qualification. One, if you are looking to get into the industry and your spouse does not qualify, are you forced to divorce so that you can get into the industry? The other, what happens if you get married after you are already in the industry and they do not qualify? These are scenarios where business planning and a competent attorney are going to be able to help you anticipate those scenarios.

One point of note on the competent attorney—we have a lot of clients who have come to us from other law firms, where a lot of attorneys have ultimately found themselves practicing in the I-502 industry, medical marijuana, or otherwise. Where they may have some experience as a criminal attorney or with minor possession, DUIs, etc., and they think they know a little bit about marijuana and feel they can assist a company with forming, developing, or even merging.

These attorneys quickly find themselves in over their heads, not because they cannot navigate or help with the administrative side of the regulations, but because planning and anticipating the business relationships and operations is a different story.

This is a novel area of the law. Recreational marijuana, which was criminal before, is now a business venture. And so all of the traditional aspects of a successful business venture such as being profitable, accounting, managing your books, hiring, labor practices, employment handbooks, dividends, securities law, etc., come into play. It is important that you find somebody who has the business understanding and general practitioner experience, not simply in an area of the law that may have previously dealt with marijuana, such as manufacture, possession, distribution, or the like, rather, I-502 and business more generally.

Typically, the primary options of an entity for moving specific business matter are an LLC or a corporation. In comparing them, the first thing that comes to mind is individual credit liability. If an individual defaults on a loan or line of credit and the creditor goes after their assets, which would include their membership interest in the LLC, this creditor ends up with an ownership interest in the company, but is not qualified by the LCB.

How is this situation going to play out? This is one of the underlying reasons the LCB has taken a position that they are not going to recognize assumptions. Because a creditor, who through judgment or otherwise, has obtained ownership of an asset through such an assumption. They have now assumed an ownership interest. The LCB is preempting that occurrence by not recognizing assumptions, thereby not jeopardizing the standing of the license.

This is just one example where business law acumen is necessary for any lawyer practicing in this industry. There are also the daily ongoing matters. Do you know all of the labor laws that you are supposed to be following for your employees? Do you understand all of your employee tax withholdings? The non-LCB things you are required to do to keep out of legal trouble.

There are securities compliance and private offering laws that must be complied with if you are issuing stock ownership or doing a private offering of the company. The laws underlying a business venture are complex and competent representation may be one of the single most important factors when running such an operation.

RIGHTS OF FIRST REFUSAL

It may become necessary at some point for a company to raise additional capital. A company that had about a million dollars to start with is now at one and a half million dollars, making them a half-million over budget. The company had to raise additional revenue, and how exactly they were going to do that was an issue. The company located investors and secured the investment with assets in the company.

To avoid forfeiture of those assets, and to attain additional capital to make it through to revenue, there were compromises and concessions that had to be made with the current investors regarding what assets were secured, limitations on the other investors, and the positions of the investors.

Similarly, from the other side of it, if you are an investor that is going into an operation that has pre-existing investors, you should consider a Purchase Money Security Interest, or PMSI. This is a tool for a particular individual to maintain priority over a specific item. The idea behind it is somebody gave a very specific amount of money for the purchase of a very specific product.

Typically a bank would have first priority on the fixtures of a property. However, a properly executed PMSI gives priority to the particular fixture to the person who provided the funds specifically for the fixture. In the event of a default, the person secured by the PMSI can go in and take the item without the bank being able to say it should get first priority.

A common example is a hardware store that sells a new stove to a homeowner on credit; the hardware store wants to make sure they have the right to repossess the stove even in the event of foreclosure on the house. Traditionally, the mortgage holder would attempt to prevent the hardware store from taking the stove because it's attached to the house—it's become affixed to the property. However, the PMSI, if properly executed, will preserve the hardware store's interest in the stove, despite being installed in the home.

Another important business and legal consideration is the Right of First Refusal ("ROFR"). This arises in a situation where a company needs to raise additional capital to purchase additional assets. Current investors may want to make sure that they have the right to invest the money first so they do not lose their position or dilute their existing interest.

Alternatively, an existing owner may want to sell its ownership interests in the company, and the company, or the other owners, may want to preserve the right to purchase it first before they sell it to somebody outside the company. This may occur for any number of reasons.

The ROFR is a provision that you would build in and it is important to provide because it allows you to have procedures and predetermined valuation methods in place. These procedures allow the company to determine what it can or cannot afford.

Another ROFR issue example is if somebody who owns the interest wants to get one million dollars for it. The company may want to preserve the right to have terms for those one million dollars, even if the terms are inferior to those of an outside party. Make sure you have a methodology for valuation—if you don't—an owner is allowed to shop for the highest bidder, despite the ROFR.

Inheritance situations present another common right of first refusal and valuation scenario. One of the valuation provisions that we drafted, for example, provided the company up to two years in an inheritance or divorce situation for the company to conduct a valuation process. The company had to write, as did the individual owner, to delay or pause the valuation for a period of time. For example, you are two months out from your first crop—either party may want to preserve the right to postpone the valuation until reaching revenue. These are things you can plan in advance with certain scenarios.

PROFESSIONAL SERVICES

Legal Expenses

There are things that individuals forget about because they think they know everything about marijuana. You have all these particular rules and regulations in play and if it is not considered you are not even going to be able to run a business. In conversations with business owners, you may ask what the biggest expenses from legal fees were.

Perhaps surprisingly, labor disputes will likely be at the top and the I-502 industry will undoubtedly be no different due to all the regulations in place. The employee handbook may be one of the single most important documents a company has as it could insulate the company from liability in the event of a rogue or non-complying employee.

Finding Competent Professional Advice

A point worth noting here is that we are dealing with such a highly specialized and nuanced area of the law, with many interworking components. At this point in time there are a limited number of firms that are highly specialized and that are taking on clients in the I-502 industry. For example, a lot of large law firms will not touch it because it may jeopardize existing contracts and clients—a large firm with a government contract is unlikely to work on I-502 matters.

It's important to find a professional—attorney and CPA—that you may want to work with because you do not want to be in a position where you have to find that person after a problem arises. You could certainly search for representation or assistance, but it is not well advertised when somebody works in the industry and this is not due to the federal status of marijuana.

Rather, people still realize it is a developing industry and many want to keep their practice diversified. Frankly, the people who have become highly specialized in the industry have needed to advertise for their reputation to spread amongst the industry.

Being involved in the industry to interact and form relationships with I-502 companies and licensees has fostered new relationships and provided new avenues for obtaining information. Everyone recognizes the value of having a certain number of people succeed in the industry and many are interested in maintaining the industry reputation as professional.

A lot of people who have been involved from the early stages in this industry recognize that this is a big opportunity. Washington State, along with Colorado, are on the cutting-edge of this industry, businesses recognize the significance of the way that they conduct their operations now, so early on in the process.

Becoming connected with other people in the community is very important. I cannot overstate the value of that.

It is another reason that working with the right professional who may be specializing in this industry can provide added benefits. A perfect example is being able to connect parties to combine resources or information. Much of the information is available, but it will be much more difficult or expensive to find that resource if you are reaching out in the industry on your own and not with the help of other industry leaders.

Attorney

If you decide to invest in this industry—you will eventually have a question about something specific to the law as it relates to I-502 or an appurtenant rule or regulation. It'll be a question that you know in advance needs to be answered right the first time. What's more, it's nice to feel confident you have received the right answer.

When that time comes—find an attorney. Most often, one or two phone calls can sort out a situation—if that phone call is made right after one or two more wrinkles has you lost in the mess, at which point, the situations becomes complicated. Most attorneys use the word complicated as a synonym for expensive.

Most of the discussion throughout this book is fairly simple, informal, intended as a guide to merely point a person in the right direction so that they are able to find a proper resource to rely on—however—the next sentence immediately after this is likely the only exception in this entire book because nowhere else have I intended, nor should you interpret or rely upon any information or statement herein as official or formal legal advice.

Here is the exception—when you eventually have that legal question I mentioned above, about something specific to I-502 and you need the right answer the first time and actually feel confident about both—my legal advice is to politely, but thoroughly challenge the competency and experience of an attorney advising you on any I-502 matter until you confirm that person's actual understanding of recreational marijuana law here in Washington State.

I won't go so far as to say that otherwise such advice is worse than no advice at all, but it might be. I have seen instances, and heard of many more, where an attorney shoots from the hip—whether due to laziness or incompetent, or both—and ultimately makes the client's situation worse than it started.

Due Diligence Services

A due diligence investigation is a great example of an instance when competency with I-502 will matter. This is when the parties to a transaction start exchanging all the information to finalize a formal agreement—it's crucial as either the incoming investor or the business accepting the investment. Requests for information must be thorough and disclosures must be complete. Usually, the most important information will be the most awkward to request—in my experience, this is not a flaw. The same self-awareness most people aspire to obtain tends to accompany an aversion to causing discomfort for others.

If for example, you're anywhere near a transaction involving the purchase or sale of an ownership interest in a company with an existing or pending I-502 license, before you even accept an offer from a potential buyer, you may need to know the person's net worth or how many times her husband has been arrested for solicitation.

The investor was interested in my client's I-502 operation. There had been no prior relationship or dealings between the parties. The potential investor offered a polished self-portrait, highlighting his most positive attributes while avoiding any specific details that could be challenged for falsity. He blustered about his business acumen and prior successful ventures. It was interesting but useless in determining his fit as an I-502 investor and LCB qualifications.

I asked how much money he was able to commit to the enterprise. He deftly avoided an exact amount by feigning financial modesty. I explained the risk my client would incur in the event the LCB withdrew their application due to disqualification of a Financier or True Party of Interest. The investor understood and explained he had access to funds ranging from $100,000 to $200,000. Note: the significant distinction lies in his careful choice of words, which kept the statement truthful.

The LCB will keep digging with indifference to the delay—patiently pushing for answers through additional requests for information over the course of weeks and months. Meanwhile, the application sits hostage to the investigation of a single applicant whose qualifications should have been confirmed long before. During this delay no other investors can enter the equation, the company cannot finalize a lease whose commencement would be indeterminable, and any other LCB related matter must be put on hold.

In qualifying an investor, the LCB's interest is to prevent the diversion of funds from illegal activities (e.g. drug cartel) into legitimate business enterprises. If the money is not yours, the LCB wants to know whose it is. That person must likewise meet all the qualification requirements—criminal background check, residency, and financial tracing. Your application will be denied due to the inclusion of unqualified persons named on the license.

In continuing my original line of questions, I asked this potential investor if he would be able to provide bank statements for at least six months with a balance representing his $100,000 to $200,000 capital investment. He could not. The funds were "available" but not deposited and not technically his own. OK, not necessarily a fact that outright precludes qualification if the funds are actually a gift or advance of inheritance.

In an under the table agreement, this is where many might rethink the arrangement—if the deal is actually a loan (so they should have been listed as a financier on the application), the lender/borrower might be OK withholding such information from the LCB, but that does not mean the lender is willing to surrender any right to recover the funds when the highly successful borrower decides that repayment is less attractive than keeping the $200,000. After all, a court of law would side with the borrower.

Was the potential investor able to provide some minimal evidence supporting any satisfactory explanation for the source of the funds? He could not. At this point, the LCB would have flatly rejected such an application. The LCB's patience will abruptly end the moment an applicant's pretended assertions are discovered.

Example Scenario 9.2

Ivan the Investor—an experienced marijuana enthusiast—has recently finished a high-profit project in a high-growth industry with an in-cash profit of $100,000. He is now looking for a legitimate investment opportunity. Popeye the Producer/Processor is the sole owner of a company with a pending application for a Tier 2 license.

Ivan offers to invest his seed money in Popeye's company by purchasing a fifty percent ownership interest. Popeye thinks $75,000 seems reasonable for such a deal. Ivan is thrilled, not only does he have enough cash to pay Popeye, but also he will still have $25,000 left for operations—jackpot! Plus, Ivan is an avid horticulturist with all the needed equipment, such as lights, pots, tools, drip lines, and a makeshift oil extractor all setup in his garage. In fact, it turns out that he remembered he also has a modest supply of soil, fertilizers, pesticides, and pretty much everything else he may need to be operational.

All of his prior undertakings were not too hard—Ivan has never bothered with taxes, paid all his laborers in cash, and had access to his friend Frank's garage, so long as Ivan shared a bit the bounty when his horticultural venture bore fruit.

Ivan does not find out until later that I-502 states that an operation cannot be operated in a location adjoined to any residence, nor did he realize the county had placed a moratorium on producer/processor activities in R2 residential zoning areas. It also turned out that the hydropower company, which is actually wholly owned by the federal government, is the only supply to their local electric utility company and consequently the utility company must refuse service to any newcomers in their service area.

Meanwhile, after the next-door neighbor perused the online list of addresses for pending marijuana applications and discovered what Ivan was planning, he rallied the whole neighborhood against Ivan. The neighborhood did not care about cost because it was a matter of principle—they would never sit by while marijuana was growing in their community.

They expected that such a business would practically invite all kinds of unsavory types of illegal activity. They argued that marijuana was now legal, and therefore, the government would be powerless to control Ivan's growing operation and police would be unable to respond to the inevitable violence, theft, or even using of marijuana that would occur in the house.

Furthermore, the neighbors could vaguely refer to many instances in which they could smell the marijuana growing in the garage and the light pollution was a nuisance. Their home values might be impaired and they also insisted they had no desire to move and would not be forced from their homes.

The neighbors did what they could to raise awareness, earning themselves a cover story on the town newspaper, which the manager of the local bank happened to read while sipping his Irish coffee waiting in line at the pharmacy. As it turned out, the bank manager also was responsible for the branch that held the mortgage on Frank's house and the mortgage terms—besides restricting commercial activities similar to the homeowner's association governing their housing development—had a strict policy against any marijuana activities on properties where they had a security interest.

Aside from the local opposition, there was also the twenty-five percent excise tax, and the numerous inspections that would be required under the city code for permitting—building electrical UL compliance, Fire Marshall, USDA, OSHA, EPA, and LCB final inspection.

Ivan finally gave up on the idea before ever pricing the new fence, security surveillance equipment, or the electric generators that would now be required for power. He had not even opened the housing associations threat to shut them off from the shared well because it was technically at a depth subjecting it to federal law, which still treats marijuana and any related activities as criminal, subjecting them to imprisonment and property seizure.

With all these considerations, no one had yet noticed the licensed daycare that sat next door, the bus stop across the street, or the public park that abutted the rear side of the property.

COMPANIES FOR SALE WITH LICENSES

It is not difficult right now to find licenses or pending applications for somebody who currently has no ties or connection to a pending license or an ongoing license. It is not difficult to find opportunities to get more involved. There are a lot of very important considerations for somebody who is looking at this industry as an option. The considerations include understanding the current status of the license.

Has the initial conversation occurred so that the license application is going to have to be amended in order to include additional investors or true parties of interest? Has the initial call to schedule that interview occurred? Is there a timeline? Have there already been delays? Has the application been amended before, so that now you are looking at a second, third, or fourth round of amendments?

As you can see, there are a lot of issues that need to be investigated and I expect a lot of people picking up this book are going to be looking at an opportunity to get involved in different parts of marijuana businesses. But the question is, do you want to become an investor during the process or wait until they already have the license and only have to amend it? Obviously the risk, the opportunities, and the potential payoffs are going to vary depending on where you enter the process.

I mentioned earlier that there is non-transferability of licenses, whether in the permit pending application stage or the final issue.

The entity itself has to retain ownership of the license. However, that does not mean the ownership of the entity itself cannot change hands.

At this point, the LCB is not processing assumptions, which means that you are actually stepping into the position of a person who may currently be listed on the license. However, that does not mean that additional interests in the entity, whether stock or membership interest, cannot be issued. The current, most common approach for investors, whether this is a business trying to get additional infusion of capital to start or maintain operations or whether it is somebody looking to get involved in the operation, is to focus on the ownership of the entity itself.

I can give you two examples. Example one; there is a retailer with its final license and has been selling product now for several months. The owner has no desire to continue operating and our client was interested in buying in. The retail operation was described as basic, and our client wanted to take a very different approach—one involving a huge investment in the design and quality of the layout.

The original licensee was interested in selling her operational business, thus highlighting one end of the buy-in spectrum. There is a concern about branding and location, and our client was interested in completely starting the business fresh, but understanding the importance of the license already being finalized. Essentially, you are adding additional people because retailers can have their name on up to three licenses. These guys are already exploring this branding/franchising-type approach.

This is a gray area. You could probably sell one-hundred percent of your business, but make sure that the original license applicant keeps some sort of interest. In the example, if the owner kept anything that prevents them from simply jumping into her shoes, then, in that situation, it is not an assumption. Alternatively, this is sometimes called an option to purchase.

Example two, is another client who has a pending Tier 2 producer/processor license, who spent months trying to find a location and raise capital, but so far have not been satisfied with the terms and people on the other side of the deals. At this point, they really just want to get out of the operation altogether.

They were willing to stay involved long enough to help facilitate getting through the licensing process. They are basically selling a controlling interest in the company—a company that is not operational and still has all the LCB requirements left to meet. This is the other end of the spectrum. It is still at that inception point.

When we got involved with them, they had not even had the phone call to schedule the initial interview with the LCB. They have since had that call and we are helping to manage the deferral of starting that process. They do not have an operation; they do not have all of the people associated with the license—yet somebody could step in and do that without any issue with the LCB.

The other way to get involved is for an investor to put up so much money and get twenty percent of the company, or something along those lines. Within the range of available ways of getting involved in the industry is the role of the investor. Do they want to be a passive investor? Do they want to be directly involved in the day-to-day operations? It varies by investor and original licensee.

Additionally, we have helped set up the financing coming in so that they can become operational and reach revenue.

The loan terms will very and often include part ownership and part repayment. It really depends on each situation and what the interests of each party are. There are a wide range of opportunities for people to enter into the market, depending on what level of involvement people want to have.

Before getting started, it would be wise to seek an attorney in order to get a feel for what may lay head. There's a good amount of time that we could spend getting into details with many of these topics and figuring out what this investment would actually mean and evaluating some of the risk. Both are limitless.

One of the biggest things, depending on where you are at this stage, is defining a realistic idea but leveling the involvement a person wants to have and what level of involvement they are competent to manage. What you do not want to end up doing is saying, "Yeah, I've got one-$100,000 I want to invest in the marijuana industry," and then find yourself running an organization where you really were looking for a more passive involvement.

The best way to avoid ending up in that type of situation is to define the level of involvement you want to have in advance, and then look for the right opportunity, rather than simply finding an opportunity and try to tailor your involvement to match the needs.

BANKRUPTCY

Bankruptcy Implications

Bankruptcy is an issue that has started to garner some attention—in part, because the intersection between state-based entity formation and contract law with federal bankruptcy law is blurry. For now, there will continue to be uncertainty for I-502 companies regarding the availability of bankruptcy protections or access to corporate reorganization options until such time when the legal status of marijuana production, possession, and sale changes at the federal level.

At the core of the bankruptcy issue: What is the federal government supposed to do? Come in and take all your marijuana plants? What are they going to do with those?

There are circumstances that may disallow marijuana businesses from using the bankruptcy court. All bankruptcy lies under the federal law administered by the federal courts. Since marijuana is a federally illegal drug, the federal courts are unable to take possession of marijuana plants or finances.

As an investor, or any individual who is contemplating any business venture, it is important to consider using your business entity as a liability protection if the worst comes, and the company fails. There may be some bankruptcy protection to get out from underneath any company debt or liability that may come as a result of the failed operation. That option is not going to be available for I-502 companies. Under state law, you will, however, still have the protections afforded to a corporate entity.

It is very important to make sure you comply with all operations following the filing date or formation of the business entity. If the business entity filing date is later than a particular action, which comes into question, or a breach of contract dispute, which arises, you are not going to have the legal protections.

Contract law falls under state law. You are going to have access to those protections that exist, which is important in light of the lack of access to the bankruptcy courts and bankruptcy laws. If a person wants to make sure that they have the legal protections available, business entities want to make sure you have complied with all the necessary steps and procedures. If you are the corporation that cannot pay, federally, there is nothing that can happen, but people could still get judgments against you for not paying.

There are two implications in this scenario. First, and most importantly, the significance of the inaccessibility of liquidation, which is the idea mentioned above that the product cannot be sold to pay creditors; and second, reorganization. The significance of the fact that bankruptcy is not available for reorganization of an entity means that if you are a company, you are not going to have the option of shedding a certain amount of the debt in order to continue operations in hopes of becoming profitable at some later point in time—to restructure the debt or financial liabilities that you may have in order to repay those in a way that will preserve the financial viability of the company while the company gets going again.

If a company is already in operation and they have debt they cannot currently bring, one option would be to bring in another investor. However, short of voluntarily negotiating a way to restructure that debt with the current debt holder, the business operator is not going to be able to force the current investor or debt holder to allow a reasonable restructure, which is what access to the bankruptcy courts would allow under reorganization.

From the investor perspective, the concept of not being able to liquidate is significant and concerning. If you, as an investor, have an abundance of money and that money has been secured by assets in the I-502 companies, it is going to be more difficult to collect on those assets. Unlike bankruptcy, where a debt holder can force the company into bankruptcy by filing on their behalf, that option is not going to be available for I-502 companies. Short of obtaining a judgment and enforcement of that judgment at a state level, forced liquidation of a company to recover your investment could be difficult.

One of our clients had an investor come in with a loan of over $500,000. As part of the loan structure, they received a security interest in the business property, and any of the tangible assets the business specifically accrued, excluding marijuana plants or products that may exist. We put provisions in there that said, "The investors are not going to be liable for the inadvertent, or even necessary destruction, or loss of any product in the course of recovering those assets." Such provisions are unique to the I-502 industry.

For example, if the investors have to come in to recoup their investment, they have to physically uproot any existing marijuana plants and dispose of them in order to get the planter pots which they can then turn around and sell. The investors are not going to be financially liable for that.

As an investor, these are some of the specific differences you want to think about before committing to an I-502 company. Conversely, if you are the business owner, you want to make sure that an investor trying to collect on a debt does not come in and destroy your entire crop, which may be the most valuable thing you have. You need another provision in there to protect you from that—one that provides for a waiting period between when the judgment is enforced and when the crop can be harvested. Business owners will want to harvest any crops before allowing their operation to be threatened by a sale of assets.

Additionally, the investor or operator may want to require some arbitration provision— a process before they attempt to collect through the courts—which may not allow for different types of protection. This is part of the business planning process that people will want to consider before they fully jump in.

The bottom line is that as an investor or business owner, you should not blindly rely on expectations that bankruptcy law or bankruptcy protections will be available as they might otherwise be for other companies. The point here is that you need to have a little more careful forethought and planning regarding potential debt default, breach, collections, security interests, and enforcement, than you might in other business operation scenarios.

You need to be able to ask yourself point blank, "How much money did you make last year? How much money do you expect to make on this each fiscal year? How much money are you bringing to the table? What kind of resources do you have?" Not everyone in his or her first conversation with someone else wants to say, "So, how many times do you have sex every week?" Hearing the question from a marriage counselor is expected and they are able to ask those types of questions soon after meeting new clients.

Similarly, an attorney is supposed to be able to help in a business relationship to establish those types of baseline measurements and to plan in advance that "prenuptial agreement," should the business relationship fail at some future point in time.

If nothing else, the impending threat of a potential bankruptcy could help you resolve some issues with creditors, or get things reorganized to keep the business going.

All of this bankruptcy discussion stems from the decision of one judge, and therefore, does not necessarily decide everything. It was a different circuit court. It was in Colorado. You cannot necessarily rely on that because it has not yet been established in Washington State.

You have to put something in the business agreement to address that failure could happen. It is an unsettled law, but this is what we have to work with. The dismissal of the case is not precedent at all. It is merely guidance of one of the decisions that has been adopted. There is specific, and likely reasonable, bankruptcy protection that is being sought in this case swept into the potential assets of the product that would have been illiquid at the federal level.

As more and more federal aspects of the government get involved, for example, the federal Indian reservations, Guam, and the IRS, you are going to start arguing that they have got their hands all over marijuana law. One reasonable expectation is that bankruptcy law may become available in the future. But products, like the marijuana crop, would remain specifically excluded from the assets that can be protected. You cannot do that for a Chapter 7 bankruptcy, where a trustee takes possession of the assets.

The recommendation would be that if an investor is hoping to secure their interest, you might want to exclude it, or else just avoid trying to secure that with a crop, which is the traditional method for agricultural operations. It is not uncommon for somebody who is providing seed to a weed grower to secure payment on that seed with a crop at a later point in time.

As an attorney, I would be loathed to advise an investor to do something like that in this case because of seizing issues. This raises a whole bunch of other related issues, such as the requirements to produce, process, and sell marijuana in Washington State. Merely, because you managed to get access to a crop does not mean that you are going to have the legal authority to process, sell, or even to take possession of the crop without having the actual license. If that license, due to some action on a part of the company, has been suspended or terminated, you may have lost the legal authority to do anything with the marijuana crop.

To my knowledge, this has not yet come up at the state level, and how exactly the state would deal with a situation where a crop is about to be harvested and the license has been terminated remains an unknown, but will undoubtedly arise at some point, likely in the next twelve months given that the LCB anticipates fifty percent of the businesses will fail.

One of the most important security interests creditors usually have is the cash collateral.

Which means they can go ahead and create and sell the product, but they cannot do anything with the cash unless you negotiate something. There is an incentive for both sides to give a little because they cannot take all the cash flow out, or there is no more incentive. A more likely scenario is the investor who has to take the crop because everything else—the property and equipment—has already been seized.

You have to be prepared, as it is a plausible scenario that the company is forced into default because they lost their license, so they can no longer legally liquidate their crop. If the company can keep their license and cash it out, it is far better for everyone, even if the company only receives a small percentage of the license value. The LCB is also taking this position.

There are so many of these questions that we face and we know are going to continue to come up at some point, but nobody necessarily has had to navigate finding a solution to it yet, so they're just unsettled.

The LCB, as mentioned before, sometimes provides conflicting answers. It depends on the interpretation, and it is such a fact-specific determination that it just depends on each scenario. It is not really clear, and you cannot always predict the way that it will go. That is why I think that having an overall strategy of making sure the LCB is on your side is going to help.

What I have noticed is that the pattern that you establish with the LCB agent from the beginning is normally going to set the tone and the mood of the interaction throughout. If you piss off that licensing agent, or you give them reason to distrust you early on, you are going to have a really difficult time in this industry. They are going to spend a lot of time investigating you because they have reason to wonder whether or not everything you are telling them is accurate.

I openly admit that as an attorney in this industry, developing my understanding is a real challenge because of how much information is not actually available. Especially with the licensing process and the LCB. As soon as they closed the licensing window, a lot of information went with that. If you try and look on their website to get some background information, really, all that you get is a web page that says the licensing window is now closed, and that is the extent of information they are willing to provide.

Whatever was there before the license lottery that told interested parties what to expect or what the process was, is no longer available. We have been able to get some of the missing information from clients, but what we have collected depends on what notes our clients still have from their initial meetings with the LCB.

There are a few driving policies behind this. One is that I do not think the LCB is prepared to be held to fixed points on a lot of this material. As an administrative agency, their responsibility is to fill in the gaps in the administration of that legal system. This is a new process and the LCB is still figuring it out. A lot of it you cannot predict exactly what is going to happen or where the problems are emerging. They have to be reactive to some of the problems in order to foster a profitable environment for marijuana.

Can an Ownership Interest be Acquired and Redistributed by Bankruptcy Trustee?

There are different types of bankruptcy, but generally in an individual bankruptcy situation, Chapter 7 or Chapter 13, there is always a trustee. The question with regard to a trustee taking ownership, to my knowledge, has not yet been answered, but this is an instance where we would have a business document to address the potential issues that could arise.

An example of a very specific provision that you need to include in an operating agreement for an I-502 company, that would not need to be included in other operating agreements for a traditional business venture, is how the transfer of ownership would occur. This would occur when an individual wants to sell their interest in order to get some of the cash out of the company and also in the event that one of the owners commits a felony and thereby disqualifies himself as a licensee.

The last thing you want to have happen is to invest $2 million into a piece of property and suddenly find you cannot sell your upcoming crop or reach first revenue because your license is suspended due to an ownership challenge. We can build provisions into agreements, which can immediately take or create a forfeiture of that person's interests, which then may be held in a trust by the company pending a decision by the other members or even a determination by the LCB regarding the qualification status of that person. The provisions that we can propose make sure the company specifically complies with any of the existing requirements regarding qualifications.

When a company evaluation is necessary, an independent appraiser, who understands enough about the market, will come in to determine the value—it is not merely a multiplier of revenue. The simple fact that a person in that venture may have just jeopardized the ability of the company to continue to operate would have a direct and immediate impact on the valuation of the company. Where a person, upon exit, might expect that each of their shares be worth $10 a piece, we can pre-build into the planning documents an automatic penalty of fifty percent of the valuation that is going to be forfeited as a direct consequence of their actions, because it is going to be defined as a breach.

One of the ways our firm has done this is by creating a default event scenario and providing a specific series of actions that are automatically going to be followed in the event of default. Because this is such a new area of the law and so many of these questions have not been answered, you do not want to be the person who sets the example of what not to do. Whomever you talk with, you have to make sure you plan for these things before you go in. This applies not only to an attorney drafting or preparing business documents or reviewing those documents but also to accounting professionals.

We, in Washington, have not gone through our first round of taxation at the federal or state level as of publication; you actually make monthly payments based on your revenue with the Department of Revenue. This process is administered by the Liquor Control Board. 2015 is the first year that license holders have made it to revenue, which means that this will be the first round of federal tax returns that are filed.

part ten

Roll it Up

NOW OR LATER?

As a law firm, I estimate that around half the time we spend on I-502 related matters is assisting clients with problems that arose before they came to us—many of which could have been avoided had we entered the picture sooner. And ninety percent of our remaining time tends to be spent planning for upcoming action. This should give you an idea about pound of cure versus an ounce of prevention.

A perfect example is all the documents we have drafted regarding inheritance. Sometimes it doesn't occur to people that clarifying not only where the money is coming from, but also the reason for the money's passing is significant. At least once, we've had to put documents together after the fact in order for the relevant parties to acknowledge that the money was not intended as a gift to the marital community, but rather for the individual as inheritance.

This is not a pitch based on our experience—it's a suggestion to make sure that whomever you are getting advice from knows to spot these kinds of issues. If they cannot handle such specialized issues, hopefully they have the foresight to refer you to somebody who can.

CLOSING REMARKS

This book is not "How to build your marijuana company," rather, it is how to ensure legal compliance, coupled with providing proper business planning. Protecting legal risk exposure and ensuring that you meet particular risks that might be affecting I-502 industries that are being considered and incorporated into any of the business documents or negotiations and terms with new investors and somebody looking to get into the industry.

The purpose of the book is to provide investors of all kinds with a broad overview of what they are going to face as they navigate the process.

Keep in mind that we have thrown in a lot of business considerations, which are general in nature, which also may not be specific to the I-502 industry. Bearing in mind that there may be people who this may be some of their first exposure to business on a scale like this. Do not take that or misinterpret that to mean that this is a comprehensive guide that addresses all of the general business type considerations that a person ought to make, but merely as a helpful resource that's providing some of those.

We also need to emphasize the fact that this certainly does not include all of the fine details of the Washington Administrative Code with regard to recreational marijuana nor does it include the details on all the appurtenant RCWs. It is safe to say this is mostly an account of the hot topics or what we most generally face and maybe some of the less understood areas.

Anyone planning to go into this should really sit down with the documents and read through them. This is not intended to replace the guidance that should be sought from a professional who is familiar with the particular issues that might be affecting businesses generally but also I-502 companies, whether tax, legal or otherwise. Nor is it intended to replace the guidance or discretion that may be exercised by the Liquor Control Board in this process.

Although we are giving a lot of examples based on our own experience with clients, this should not be relied on as an absolute authority on how exactly the LCB may interpret a situation based on specific facts. The LCB may choose to change its policy or regulations at any time. A lot of this information is very time specific and a person reviewing this ought to be aware that on a weekly basis some of these regulations, policies, approaches, etc., are changing.

A significant example is a couple of months ago the LCB issued emergency rules regarding packaging. Providing some additional clarification on what types of packaging were permissible and which type is not, in the wake of an incident in Colorado where there was a death following consumption of an edible. Significant changes are occurring at any time, so do not use the information in this book as a substitute for seeking guidance, but merely as a guide to address some of the issues.

It is probably safe to say that while we provide a lot of the issues that we faced and provide some very general answers, our advice would be, if you do face any of these similar issues, to seek professional advice on the issue. Every situation is going to be fact specific.

It might be better to look at this from the perspective that we may be providing some examples of red flags that may not have come to your attention, that may need to be investigated further, but not necessarily a comprehensive list of what those red flags might be. Forecasting, budget, and planning are all things to keep in mind.

First, be prepared for the licensing process to take longer than you might hope. Twelve months is a reasonable, if not conservative, estimate. The fastest I have seen somebody move through, start to finish, and have everything lined up, was approximately three months.

Forecast, be prepared, and build a comfortable cushion. Be prepared throughout that entire timeline to have the capital to pay for both expected and unexpected fees, whether legal fees, penalty fees, permitting fees, or otherwise.

That is the biggest reason that people are experiencing budget and cost overruns from their original forecast. They were not prepared for potential time-delay obstacles, often due to location setbacks. Common pitfalls are more widely known today, but depending on where an applicant is in the process, problems may still arise. The people who have experienced the most financial hardship were those who really were not prepared.

There are going to be some situations, although I hope we are past them, that you simply cannot prepare for and may not be able to overcome. It is not something we have experienced, but how does one who has $600,000, $800,000, or even a million dollars invested in a property before final licensing overcome being zoned out of the property by the county?

Fighting a legal battle may be the only recourse, but this is where doing your due diligence is so important. It is the thing that is going to save a lot of time and money, which is why it was emphasized so heavily when discussing land use and finding a location. There may be the one-off situation where someone is zoned out and you could not prepare for it, but proper due diligence will alleviate most issues.

Whether the business is a startup or an ongoing concern, the people running successful companies most often point to three key relationship that have significant bearing on the management of the business operations: their attorney, accountant, and banker—the I-502 industry is no exception. In fact, given the particularly strict regulations governing licensing, financial disclosure and banking restrictions, these relationships will be even more crucial to establish early, before you run into problems.

A DISCLAIMER ON SCOPE OF THIS BOOK

As we near the end, please note the following final disclaimer regarding the scope of this book. This book and the subject matter it covers is not intended as an end-all for any person to rely solely upon whether or not such subject matter or any particular issue is addressed briefly or at length for any particular situation. The amount of time or space dedicated to any topic in this book is not intended as a commentary on the relative importance of the topic covered. There may be important considerations that apply to your situation which are beyond the scope of this book or simply were not covered in depth or even omitted altogether. Please consult a professional before making any decisions that could impact your financial or legal standing, including but not limited to decisions regarding the best course for proceeding through the license approval process or successfully establishing the profitability of your venture.

This book is intended as an initial primer and basic introduction to some of the more common issues people have encountered—this is not by any means an exhaustive or fully comprehensive treatise on the subject matter covered, nor does this book touch upon or mention every major or minor issue that may apply to your particular situation. Many of the topics discussed above were selected in order to draw the reader's attention to an issue that was once overlooked by at least one person—whether or not such an oversight led to a substantive problem for that person is typically a product of how long it took to make an appropriate course correction.

Importantly, the purpose of this book is not to propose any single solution or a finite list of potential options to any of the situations discussed—instead, the purpose of this book is to encourage the reader to seek additional guidance if any of the issues discussed has any relevance to the reader's situation. This does not necessarily mean that any discussion of the issues presented above is incomplete, but that every person's situation will have unique circumstances and facts that may significantly impact the outcome of a particular issue in a way that is not mentioned nor anticipated in the above discussion.

Also be wary of the danger that accompanies the increasingly popular, though often mistaken, assumption regarding the quality, reliability, or even availability of answers and explanations available online. It is especially difficult to ascertain the credibility or dependability of information in an area of law that is evolving as quickly as it is here in the recreational marijuana arena. Simply searching the internet and applying the solution that pops up will consistently provide unpredictable results. Due to the newness of the law governing this industry, often the best, most appropriate solution is ultimately as new as the law to which it relates—consequently, even in those case where an online or second-hand solution seems adequate, such shortcuts often cost more in time or money, or unnecessary risk posed to the license or financial viability of the company. Please take the time to consult a qualified professional or expert early on in order to avoid an avoidable crisis later.

In writing this book, other attorneys and resources have been consulted. For a partial list of these resources, please refer to the acknowledgments section—you may also contact the author; at the very least, I can usually help point a person in right direction.

Made in the USA
San Bernardino, CA
25 June 2015